RITUAL, MYTH AND MAGIC IN EARLY MODERN EUROPE

Ritual, Myth and Magic in Early Modern Europe

WILLIAM MONTER
Professor of History,
Northwestern University, Illinois

Ohio University Press
Athens, Ohio

Ohio University Press
Athens, Ohio

© 1983 by William Monter

All rights reserved. Published 1984

Printed in Great Britain

Library of Congress Catalog Card Number 83-043136

ISBN 0-8214-0762-7

For Rosellen

Jesus, my brethren, was not superstitious or intolerant; he said not a single word against the cult of the Romans, who surrounded his country. Let us imitate his indulgence, and deserve to experience it from others.

(Voltaire, *On Superstition*)

CONTENTS

Tables

ACKNOWLEDGEMENTS

Three historians have, in very different ways, contributed most to the making of this book. A paper given by T.K. Rabb at the American Historical Association meeting in 1981 offered a bold way to re-think the problem of religious toleration in early modern Europe on broader grounds than usual. Many conversations with John Tedeschi, who was remarkably generous with references and unpublished materials, opened up the world of the Roman Inquisition in particular and the Mediterranean systems in general. Finally, the cheerful nudging and exemplary breadth of Geoffrey Parker made him an ideal patron for this project. To each of them, my thanks.

In prefaces, families are always accommodating and spouses always patient yet critical for the authors' benefit. Mine truly were, and my wife richly deserves her dedication.

W.M.

PROLOGUE

The policy of the Emperors and the Senate, so far as it concerned religion, was happily seconded by the reflections of the enlightened, and by the habits of the superstitious, parts of their subjects. The various modes of worship which prevailed in the Roman world, were all considered by the people as equally true; by the philosopher, as equally false; and by the magistrate, as equally useful. And thus toleration produced not only mutual indulgence, but even religious concord.

Thus spoke Edward Gibbon, at the outset of the second chapter of his renowned *Decline and Fall of the Roman Empire*, painting an idealised portrait of the second century Stoic emperors. It is a standard picture of what the *philosophes* of the Enlightenment understood by 'toleration' and by 'superstition', which in turn is reasonably close to contemporary usage.

Three different lines of inquiry run out from Gibbon's remark. The first is etymological: both 'superstition' and 'toleration' are Latinate words, but it is not easy to understand why the former should have pejorative connotations, while the latter had come to be a virtue by Gibbon's day. 'Superstition' is derived from words meaning 'standing above', whereas 'toleration' comes from a verb meaning 'to endure' or 'to bear', especially pain. Yet from its earliest appearance in the first century BC, 'superstition' was used patronisingly by Roman authors to refer to inaccurate divination or, in the case of Cicero, who gave the first etymology of the word, useless religious practices, and scholars who have traced the word through Roman antiquity notice a continuously increasing pejorative denotation to the term, a process capped by the triumphant Christians of the fourth century who extended it to a vast range of traditional religious practices. Its Greek counterpart, fixed by Plutarch in the age before Gibbon's Stoic emperors, similarly acquired overtones close to those of our *OED*: beliefs or practices

1

resulting from ignorance, or from unreasoning fear of the unknown or mysterious; unnecessary or superfluous religious practices, especially those which rely on magic. At the same time, 'toleration' had already become something praiseworthy by the age of the second-century emperors: a typically Roman virtue, flinty and patronising, even a little painful to the tolerator, but official policy to be upheld because it promoted the *pax Romana*. Many of the practices thus 'tolerated' were in fact 'superstitions'.[1]

The second line of inquiry leads from Gibbon back to his subject, the religious policies of Rome at its territorial zenith. Were they truly able to promote and enforce permissive or liberal attitudes towards religious beliefs and customs differing from the official state religion? Under what provocations did the Romans become intolerant? Was there, in other words, a golden age of religious toleration somewhere back in the pre-Christian Roman past, which disappeared after the triumph of Christianity, and could not be recaptured even during the revival of classical thought known as the Renaissance? How does Gibbon's portrait of the tolerant Stoic emperors fit with the well-known and widespread persecution of Christians before the conversion of Constantine early in the fourth century?

Modern scholarship agrees that the second-century Roman empire opposed some religions for clearly-defined reasons. Either its rituals were considered shockingly licentious and immoral; or it was accused of sacrificing human beings; or it interfered with Roman administration or the practice of the Roman state religion. Gibbon himself observed in his second chapter that 'under the specious pretext of abolishing human sacrifices' the early Julio-Claudians suppressed the power of the Druids in Gaul. The painfully slow acceptance of the cult of Isis, whose altars were destroyed no fewer than five times in Rome itself before the early Julio-Claudians began favouring her, demonstrates that some pre-Christian mystery cults from the East had considerable trouble gaining toleration from the Roman state, even though they did not oppose Rome's official religion.[2] Finally, and most pertinently, there is the example of the Jews, from whom the Christians descended. When it expanded into the eastern Mediterranean, the Roman state ordinarily continued Hellenistic policies of official protection, separate taxation, much autonomy, and some special privileges for Jews. Much of this changed after the Zealots led a revolt against Roman rule in 66 AD which ended with the destruction of Jerusalem and the accelerated scattering of the Jews throughout the Roman world. There was a second Jewish war (130–4 AD) when groups of Jews tried to capture the new city built on the site of Jerusalem. But even afterwards, Rome excused the Jews from worshipping the reigning emperor, and they remained a licensed religion who paid a special head tax to Rome. In the major cities of the empire were assimilationist Jews who had acquired full Roman citizenship while practising their religion. 'According to the maxims of universal toleration', said Gibbon in his famous chapter on the rise of Christianity, 'the Romans protected a superstition [Judaism] which they despised.' The uneasy, edgy coexistence between Judaism and the Roman empire after the fall of Jerusalem was also the basic model for Roman policies towards the early Christians. Both Jews and Christians suffered once during the first century: Caligula tried to have his statue placed in the Temple at Jerusalem; Nero blamed the Christians for the great fire of Rome. But most of the time, as demonstrated by a note of Hadrian to a proconsul in Asia, the Roman state accepted creeds which remained rigidly opposed to its official religion and to the worship of its emperors. All Christian martyrdoms before the third century were the result of popular rioting rather than state policy.[3]

So far, Gibbon's portrait seems reasonably accurate. But what of 'superstition'? Gibbon himself, of course, was well aware that the Roman state practised a religion which relied heavily on such practices as auguries from the entrails of sacrificed animals. His description of second-century Stoic officials as 'sometimes condescending to act a part on the theatre of superstition', where 'they concealed the sentiments of an atheist under the sacerdotal robes', is overdrawn and misleading. It seems certain that astrology and many other magical practices played an important part in the decisions of nearly all Roman subjects from emperors down to slaves. Unofficial religions were 'tolerated', i.e., endured and put up with so long as they were not actively dangerous; divination and related magical practices were an accepted part of everyday life, satirists notwithstanding. Roman law, the proudest achievement of a vast and long-lived empire, never envisioned decrees against the practice of magic as such, but only against magic which had demonstrably caused harm to man or beast. There were some famous prosecutions for harmful spells in the first century, described by Tacitus and Suetonius, and more in the early fourth century. Although 'superstition' was ridiculed by some *literati*, Roman public opinion as a whole apparently believed in its efficacy and assumed its lawfulness unless it threatened life or limb. The Romans punished harmful magic precisely because it was effective, never because it was 'superstitious'.[4]

The third line of inquiry thus leads from Gibbon's assessment of second-century Roman religious toleration and superstition up to Gibbon's own time. Was he merely reading back the practices and attitudes of some of his Enlightenment contemporaries into the Roman past? Had Europe's ruling classes truly achieved religious toleration and destroyed religious superstitions by 1770? It seems quite logical to assume that they had done neither. One need look no further than Gibbon's own England, which refused the privileges of university education and parliamentary representation to both Catholic and Protestant minorities and which, unlike second-century Rome, refused to allow native-born Jews the full privileges of its citizenship. The ruling class of Gibbon's England does seems to have shunned 'superstition'; they surpassed the Romans when they repealed their laws against harmful witchcraft in 1736. But the rustics of Hanoverian England still lynched at least one witch in Gibbon's lifetime. If English kings had abandoned their thaumaturgical powers by Gibbon's day, the lower classes still read astrological almanacs and cheerfully continued a great many forms of magical folklore. On the whole, Gibbon's and Voltaire's contemporaries seem perhaps less superstitious, but also less tolerant than the Stoic emperors. It is the purpose of these essays to tell us how they got that way, beginning around 1500, shortly after the discovery of the Americas and the expulsion of the Jews from Spain and their forced mass conversion in Portugal, with the development of printing (used not only for the critical Christian humanism of Erasmus, but also for the complete guide to witch-hunting, the *Malleus Maleficarum*), and shortly before the beginning of the Protestant Reformation posed the issue of religious toleration in novel and important ways within Christendom. We shall attempt to draw some fresh diagonals through reasonably well-explored terrain in early modern Europe.

Notes

1 See D. Grodzynski, '"Superstitio"', *Revue des études anciennes*, 76 (1974), 36–60; L. Janssens, 'Die Bedeutungsentwicklung von superstitio/superstes', *Mnemosyne*, 28 (1975), 135–89. Plutarch's essay 'On Superstition' is in the Loeb Classical Library edition of his *Moralia*, ii, 451–95.

2 R.E. Witt, *Isis in the Greco-Roman World* (Ithaca, 1971).

3 See especially E. Mary Smallwood, *The Jews under Roman Rule* (Leiden, 1976); and J.N. Sevenster, *The Roots of Pagan Antisemitism in the Ancient World* (Leiden, 1975).

4 The most persuasive approach to this subject is Julio Caro Baroja, *The World of the Witches* (Chicago, 1965), 17–40; also F.H. Cramer, *Astrology in Roman Law and Politics* (Philadelphia, 1954).

1 POPULAR PIETY IN LATE MEDIEVAL EUROPE

Christendom in 1500 was a coherent cultural unit, with enough overall uniformity to make a general description possible, and enough regional differences in popular religion to make such a description partially invalid almost anywhere. A network of hundreds of bishoprics and tens of thousands of parishes blanketed Europe from Portugal to Poland, from Scotland to Dalmatia. Dotted among them were thousands of monastic convents, both the older houses in rural districts and the newer mendicant houses in nearly every town of over 4000 inhabitants. Not only was Europe united in obedience to the Roman Pope, but it was also provided with an adequate (probably a superabundant) supply of clergy, both secular and regular. The density of clergy per thousand population was about five times as great as in the most heavily Catholic regions of Europe today.[1]

Penetrating beneath this heavy clerical layer to the religious beliefs and customs of the Christian laity in 1500 is not easy. There is however an emerging consensus about some of its more important features. In the most intensively studied late medieval region, Germany, recent scholarship insists on its pervasive 'churchliness', claiming that 'there has hardly been an age in the second millenium of Church history which offered less resistance to the dogmatic absolutism of the Catholic church'.[2] The deep piety of 1500 found expression in new religious brotherhoods, new festivals, new processions, new church buildings. By 1500 the Papacy had overcome the crisis of confidence it had suffered during the Great Schism and the Conciliar epoch; doctrinal heresy was either contained in Bohemia, or in decline. The new forms of popular devotion were either directly encouraged by priests and friars, or at any event were not in overt conflict with them. The picture drawn for Germany, where scholarship has long concentrated on late medieval religious practices because of their connections with the Reformation, seems basically valid elsewhere.

Although the intensity and even the orthodoxy of late medieval popular devotion seem well-established, the quality of popular religious practices, and especially of popular religious education, is far more questionable. In some respects, current scholarship here is still dominated by such great syntheses as Johann Huizinga's *Waning of the Middle Ages* (1924) or Emile Mâle's *Religious Art in France at the End of the Middle Ages* (1926). Both underlined the exaggerated and sometimes grotesque character of fifteenth-century Christianity, particularly those forms designed for mass consumption; Huizinga spoke on one page of its 'hyperbolic humility', 'excessive humility' and 'fantastic humility'. Art historians are not often kind towards an age whose giants, Matthias Grünwald or Hieronymous Bosch, are uncongenial to rational or optimistic minds, and historians of literature have not been much kinder to their late Gothic counterparts. Even the synthesis of German 'churchliness' in 1500 complains about its 'trend towards wild and . . . violent excitement, an inclination to simplify and vulgarise the holy' and about its lack of originality.[3]

Religious art and the literature of spirituality are not our only guides, and perhaps not our best possible guides, to exploring the world of fifteenth-century popular religion. Twenty years ago, a student of religious practice in late medieval Flanders used parish financial records to discover their most popular holidays. Measured by the amount of donations given, Good Friday easily led the list, followed by Easter, Christmas, and Pentecost. Measured by the 'ablutions' of wine given to parishioners at major festivals, Easter came far ahead of anything else; Christmas stood a distant second, getting scarcely one-fifth the attendance of Easter; while other holidays trailed close behind. Easter was the only season when parishioners were required to take communion, which in turn required them to make a formal confession sometime between Ash Wednesday and Palm Sunday; only excommunicates (who were quite numerous in Flanders) avoided these obligations. Christendom in 1500 may have been both orthodox and observant, but most Flemings stayed away from mass on most Sundays and most other holy days. Only the Lenten season, and its climax on Holy Week, truly mattered for popular religion – but they were vital.

They were also surrounded by various vanished beliefs and customs. During Holy Week, for example, Flemings avoided paying debts in any multiple of 30 pence. Even more special customs had grown up around Christmas, where folklore had begun to create its own pious songs (although the most famous symbol of this lore, the Christmas tree, was almost unknown even in extremely pious and ceremonial Germany during the late middle ages). In Flanders, people believed in a 'Hell-cart' or bloody chariot (*bloewagen*) filled with drunken demons spewing fire and blood, angrily roaming the skies for twelve days after the Incarnation. As the abbé who investigated late medieval Flanders noted, 'the incredible survival of Germanic folklore, inclinations towards superstitions . . . show how far the pagan base of this people remained an undeniably close substratum; the Bronze Age and the Iron Age survived into the age of the manuscript and the miniature'.[5]

Records of episcopal visitations, which offer much evidence about lay religious practices in the period after the Council of Trent, are of little use in this respect before 1500. At most they can tell us about the shortcomings of parish clergy as seen by the visiting inspectors, but the parishioners rarely played an important role. In so far as their voices can be heard, the laity seemed only to desire a prompt and correct celebration of mass and administration of the sacraments, and an adequate concern for church property. They never complained about a priest's ignorance, or even about his concubine, if he had one; indeed they would sometimes try to hide her from the outside inspectors.[6]

Although it is true that the beliefs and practices of ordinary fifteenth-century Christians are difficult to grasp in their totality, and although they frequently struck either a contemporary reformer like Erasmus or modern commentators both Protestant and Catholic as extremely superstitious, we must not paint too dark a picture. On the other side of the ledger is the religious education of one fifteenth-century Christian with a rural background, unshakeable orthodoxy and remarkable clear-headedness about the fundamentals of her faith: Joan of Arc. This peasant girl from Lorraine had been taught her basic prayers – the Paternoster, the Ave Maria, and the Credo – by her mother, rather than her parish priest, and in French rather than in Latin. She knew enough to distinguish between her obligatory confession to her parish priest during Lent, and the special confessions she occasionally made to visiting friars. Similarly, she could distinguish between an apparition, like St Michael or St Catherine, and a fairy, which she insisted she had never seen. She had helped the girls of her village prepare 'hats' of flowers in honour of the Virgin, a distant ancestor of the Rosary. She went to mass daily, which marks her as unusually devout. But when she burst onto the public stage in 1429, she was still completely illiterate; Joan of Arc received her religious formation entirely from her family, rather than from priests or from the Bible.[7]

A numerous clergy, trying to administer rituals accurately but not to explain their meaning, preaching about morality rather than dogma, lived among a population which was both devout and indiscriminating about the boundaries between the sacred and the profane. The vigour and virulence of the Christian humanist critique of current religious practices which burst upon Germany and much of Christendom just after 1500 shattered the Indian summer of late medieval piety. Erasmus's cry in the *Enchiridion* that *monachatus non est pietas* truly was the sixteenth-century version of Voltaire's *écrasez l'infâme*! But the Christian humanists, like the *philosophes*, never foresaw the political consequences of their attacks. If we envision the Erasmians as a shrill minority with some élite support, they become indirect guides, by antithesis, to the ordinary piety of their age, which included large doses of myth, miracle and magic. Bearing in mind the immense gulf between popular religion and humanist perspectives, and bearing in mind Luther's reply to Erasmus that scholarship is not piety, let us explore some of the salient features of this late medieval popular Christianity.

First, it was devoted to the miraculous powers of the Virgin Mary, even more than to her crucified son. Although it is true that Marian devotion began in the high middle ages, it is important to appreciate how much this fashion increased during the later middle ages. If we consider the problem of miracle-working shrines, for example, we find that the best of the oldest ones, typified by St James of Compostella, were built over the bones of a widely-known saint. But by the later middle ages, particularly in areas like northern Germany or southern Castile which had been Christian-ised by force and which had few indigenous saints, the numbers of shrines devoted to Mary after 1100 were huge. It is no coincidence that the three great national shrines developed during the fifteenth century – an age with a relatively small crop of fresh saints – were all Marian: Our Lady of Walsingham in England, which attracted more pilgrims than St Thomas Becket's Canterbury shrine by the 1530s; Our Lady of Guadeloupe in Spain, which was similarly outstripping St James after 1500; and Our Lady of Altötting in Bavaria, which became the 'national' shrine for the empire in the 1490s. (Flanders may have missed its 'national' Marian shrine when an image of her suspended from a cherry tree burned down in 1459 after four years of activity and over 300 recorded miracles.) The vast survey of imperial pilgrimage shrines by Lionel Roth-krug gives the fullest picture of the late medieval Marian surge, which seems especially pronounced in southern Germany (Bavaria, Franconia, Austria, Swabia, and Baden):

Table 1.1 *Types of south German shrines, 1000–1530*

Date	Mary (%)	Christ (%)	Saints (%)
pre-1200	20 (15)	16 (12)	94 (82)
1200 – 1360	55 (42)	24 (18)	53 (40)
1360–1530	242 (49)	58 (12)	192 (39)

In the rest of Germany, where indigenous saints were even rarer, Christ remained as popular as Mary until 1360, but afterwards the Virgin accounted for nearly 60 per cent (118 of 203) of all new shrines.[8]

Spanish evidence confirms the importance of Mary. In a detailed survey of New Castile in the 1570s, only about a third (277 of 871) chapels or *ermitas* were dedicated to her. Only fifty-three of these had witnessed any miraculous cures, but more than two-thirds of such *ermitas* were dedicated to the Virgin; finally, all but two of the fourteen shrines which had drawn pilgrims from distant villages were hers. The important Marian shrines of New Castile were clustered in places south of the Tagus river, in an area conquered from the Moors only during the thirteenth century. North of the Tagus were twenty-six major shrines to Mary or to her mother, and twenty to other saints; south of the Tagus were twenty-seven shrines to Mary or Anne, and only three to other saints. Nearly a dozen of the southern Marian shrines were located in castles built by the *conquistadores*; eight of them were known as 'Our Lady of the Castle'. There was a similar knightly flavour to late medieval Marian piety in Bavaria, where eighteen of her shrines were associated with miracles performed during the hunt, and where a special type of shrine, the *schöne Maria*, were built over the site of a synagogue after a massacre or expulsion of the Jews.[9]

Of course, late medieval Marian piety usually took less warlike and less aristocratic forms. The early fourteenth-century *Mater dolorosa* persisted over the next few centuries, taking such forms as the seventy-plus shrines to the 'Suffering Mary' in the Holy Roman Empire, or in the late fifteenth-century Flemish devotion to the Seven Sorrows of the Virgin, founded by a parish priest. The crowns of flowers which Joan of Arc and her companions wove in honour of Mary were later followed by organised 'crowns' of prayers, ten Hail Marys alternating with one Our Father, which became the devotion of the Rosary. Vigorously promoted by the Dominicans, Confraternities of the Rosary mushroomed during the second half of the fifteenth century. Their most important German organiser, Jacob Sprenger, also wrote the most important handbook on witch-hunting, the *Malleus Maleficarum*. In Spain, *ermitas* dedicated to the Rosary multiplied rapidly during the sixteenth century, and outnumbered those to any saint except Sebastian by the 1570s. This form of Marian piety was especially congenial to women, who could more easily display their devotion through prayer than by founding costly altars or chapels. In yet another way, women, children and men of humble condition showed their special allegiance to the Virgin by reporting visions of her more often than of Christ or any of the saints, at least in Spain (then, as in more recent times, such reports were carefully checked out by ecclesiastical authorities before authentication).[10]

Popular devotion to the Son lagged well behind his Mother, although Jesus was vastly more popular than any individual saint. Across northern Germany, from Westphalia to Pomerania and Prussia, forty new shrines were dedicated to Christ, but only eight to the saints between 1360 and 1530. Late medieval devotion to Jesus was heavily concentrated on the crucifix or on the prone corpse of the *Pietà*, while the mature Jesus – teaching, preaching, working miracles – was rarely envisaged. (A fifteenth-century Flemish painting showed the infant Jesus, held on Mary's right arm, writing on a tablet.) Typically, Jesus was worshipped through veneration of numerous fragments of the Cross or the Crown of Thorns; through shrines of the Holy Blood, as at Bruges or Hailes in England; or even through wonder-working images of the Man of Sorrows (*Schmerzensmannsbilder*) in Bavaria. Jesus had one new feast day in the later middle ages, Corpus Christi, which seems to have been less popular than some of the Virgin's festivals such as Candlemas, the Annunciation or the Assumption.

The role of the saints in late medieval popular devotion is not easy to grasp. They had largely lost their earlier role as miracle workers, and relatively few new saints were created during the fifteenth century. For instance, England, which had a half dozen new saints in the thirteenth century, had only one in the fifteenth century; Joan of Arc seems utterly different from other female saints of her century (mostly aristocratic, visionary nuns) and in any case was not canonised until 1920. The saints survived in a formal capacity in the names of ordinary Christians: in the 1400s, pagan names were dying out on the northern and eastern fringes of Christendom, and classical names were just beginning their vogue among élite groups in Renaissance Italy. But in one important respect saints continued to serve as a focus for local popular piety. They still dominated the flock of local *ermitas* in Castile and the lay confraternities of both northern and southern France. Around 1500, half the *confréries* of Champagne were named for therapeutic saints, and the same was true at Avignon. Everywhere the most popular saint was Sebastian, who together with St Roch protected against the plague.[11]

In the Christendom of 1500 there was no great gap between popular piety and the religion of the élite. In England, the shrine of Our Lady of Walsingham was visited on pilgrimages by the Duke of Buckingham, Cardinal Wolsey, and even Erasmus in the early 1500s; Katherine of Aragon provided for a pilgrimage to it in her will, and even Henry VIII paid for a candle there in March 1538, just a few months before his government ordered her statue taken to London and destroyed. The Emperor Frederick III visited Altötting in 1491, early in its miraculous phase. His sixteenth-century successor, Charles V, resigned all his dignities to end his life as a hermit; while his son Philip II removed one thorn from a relic Crown to put by the bedside of his sick son.[12] Pilgrimages, miracles, relic-worship, even ritual flagellation in the case of

Charles v at Yuste – such late medieval phenomena were for royalty as much as peasants.

However, it is not true that Christendom in 1500 was totally uncritical about its miracles, even before Erasmus and the early Protestants began attacking relics and pilgrimages. The best-known example of a bogus miracle unmasked by ordinary people was the Jetzer affair at Bern in 1509. The local Dominicans, propagators of the Rosary cult, exploited a visionary novice in order to stage a miracle by the Virgin which was directed against the Franciscan doctrine of the Immaculate Conception. Jetzer saw a host turn bloody, received the stigmata, and a picture of the Virgin in his room began to weep bloody tears. But the whole business unravelled when Jetzer began contradicting himself and soon turned state's evidence; he implicated four Dominican brothers whom the magistrates arrested, tortured, and condemned to death for sacrilege, heresy, and dealings with the Devil. Jetzer was merely defrocked and banished, subsequently marrying, and working as a tailor.[13]

Jetzer drew the inspiration for his visions from a recently painted 'Mass of the Dead' near the altar of Bern's main church. Historians of art and literature have been struck by the late fifteenth-century preoccupation with death at a time when demographers argue that the population was rising rapidly over most of western Europe. Regardless of demographic realities, there was certainly a spate of treatises on the art of dying well, and an enormous vogue of pictorial Dances of Death over much of transalpine Europe in the late 1400s, reflecting enormous anxiety about the fate of souls after death. The rapid spread of the doctrine of purgatory produced a huge multiplication of commemorative masses for the dead, and a rapidly growing trade in indulgences on behalf of sinners languishing in purgatory. All these developments are interconnected.

In a famous passage, Huizinga claimed that 'at the close of the Middle Ages the whole vision of death may be summed up in the word *macabre*, in its modern meaning'. He traced the word itself to a poem of 1376, where it was associated with the idea of a dance, and observed that 'the idea of the death-dance is the central point of a whole group of connected conceptions'.[14] By the time the *Danse Macabre* was published in 1485, dozens of illustrations of its major theme were already scattered across northern Europe. On a few occasions, as at Basel in 1439 or at Lübeck in 1463, these Dances of Death were commissioned as the direct consequence of an attack of plague, but for the most part they needed no such stimulus. Besides the dancing skeletons were putrefying skeletons depicted on many fifteenth-century tombstones (the entombment of Christ was also a popular French motif), or even the skeletal priests who celebrated the Mass for the Dead in Jetzer's Bern (after the 1509 trials, they were judged too realistic and had flesh painted on them).

Closely connected with this preoccupation with death was the rapid spread of belief in purgatory during the later middle ages. In the thirteenth century, mendicant friars had preached against the popular belief that souls went directly either to heaven or hell after death. In southern France, where this phenomenon has been most carefully mapped, the habit of accumulating *post mortem* masses in order to speed the soul's journey through purgatory became widespread only after 1350. By the fifteenth century a picture of purgatory could be found between panels representing heaven and hell on a roadside chapel in Provence. After 1350 poor and rich alike tried to accumulate masses to help their souls through purgatory. Peasants seldom stockpiled masses, but remained faithful until the nineteenth century to a simple system of commemoration on the ninth day after death and the first anniversary. Burghers, merchants and artisans accumulated hundreds and even thousands of *post mortem* masses: 'accounting for years of purgation, like mercantile accounting, was cumulative rather than repetitive; it doubtless contributed towards exorcising the old fears of Hell, without completely calming newer 15th-century anxieties about the decomposition of bodies'. The systems employed were quite ingenious, and defy easy tabulation. Around Avignon, where thousands of post-1350 wills document this phenomenon, even poorer people had sets of five masses in honour of the five wounds of Christ, or seven to commemorate the seven joys of the Virgin. In 1488 a rural notable commissioned twelve, seven, ten, eleven and forty masses in honour of the Apostles, the seven orders of angels, the 10,000 martyrs, the 11,000 virgins, and the 40,000 Holy Innocents. But quantity was often more important than symbolism. By the fifteenth century, small town notables were commissioning several perpetual anniversary masses. At the same time, more traditional forms of pious bequests declined.

Around Avignon almost nobody subsidised *post mortem* pilgrimages for their soul's sake, and gifts to traditional charities fell off quite sharply in the 1400s.[15]

Hastening souls through purgatory to paradise required more, or less, than commemorative masses; the most popular new form of posthumous aid developed during the later middle ages was undoubtedly the papally-authorised indulgence. The scale of this business in 1500 is justifiably notorious. Of course, there was Cardinal Albert of Brandenburg collecting relics worth a total of 39, 245, 120 years, about which Tetzel later preached and against which Luther scoffed. A much prized form of indulgence was a jubilee, a remission of *all* time in purgatory caused by all sins committed up to the present. Such plenary indulgences were offered by popes to pilgrims visiting Rome on certain jubilee years, starting in 1300. By the early 1500s, they could also be found in other parts of Christendom. The oldest jubilee in Spain, for example, was started by King Ferdinand's ambassador to Rome in favour of a hospital. It was so successful that enough money was left over to rebuild a monastery in the same town. Partial indulgences were granted for a wide variety of good works: one of the odder instances was a three-year indulgence offered by Charles v and the Pope to anyone contributing to restore the dikes of Holland and Flanders after a disastrous flood in 1515, which brought in over 128,000 ducats. Such huge profits suggest that demand was at least as great as supply in the indulgence trade. Not some sinister conspiracy between princes and popes, but genuine popular anxieties lay behind this phenomenon. The real attractions of indulgences can be glimpsed in the will of an Avignon couple in 1466, who were to be buried in white garments with four red and two green cushions on which their letters of indulgence were to be placed. The monks who buried them retrieved the cushions, but kept the letters with the corpses.[16]

Another aspect of popular religion and its preoccupation with death which flourished in the later middle ages were religious confraternities. Beyond their special devotions to a particular saint or a special cult, these voluntary associations seems to have functioned to a considerable extent as burial societies for their members. Virtually unknown in 1300 because of their communal and revolutionary overtones, these brotherhoods or *confratrias* grew remarkably during the fifteenth century. In northern

Germany, Lübeck had no fewer than seventy of them before the Reformation, Cologne eighty, and Hamburg (population 13,000) over a hundred, mostly recent foundations. Sixteenth-century Castile averaged about one brotherhood per hundred households in town and countryside alike. The pious confraternity was an unusually flexible institution, both in its membership and its functions. It was open in theory to anyone of 'good fame', to women as well as men, to rich as well as poor: the confraternity of Our Lady of Thuin at Ypres in 1426 included lame, blind, deaf and poor people along with rich burghers, and met once a week for a special mass. Other confraternities might do anything from staging a morality play, to commemorating a voyage to Compostella, to subsidising a new set of stained-glass windows for their parish church. Moreover, they were non-exclusive: one could have multiple memberships, just like modern fraternal societies. The record for excess joining was held by a Saxon official who belonged to three dozen, but some, otherwise ordinary, people in places like Avignon or Champagne often belonged to half a dozen. As its name suggests, the *confratria* of 1500 was a moral community, a kind of artificial extended family whose members were expected to attend each others' funerals and remember them in their prayers. These institutions were encouraged by the friars, but were not yet closely controlled by the local clergy, as they would become in post-Tridentine Catholicism. They did not yet have branches specialising in flagellation, those penitential brotherhoods of Mediterranean Europe which King Henry III would try to introduce to Paris in the 1580s. In 1500, religious confraternities were genuinely popular movements which provide a valuable measure of grassroots piety among the Christian laity.[17]

Like Mariolatry, anti-semitism is often perceived as a product of the high middle ages, yet it too reached its fullest developments only after 1350. It is true that German pogroms date back to the First Crusade, that Christian belief in the ritual murder of a young Christian by Jews dates from 1144 in England, and that the Lateran Council of 1215 first proposed that Jews wear distinctive yellow badges – but all these developments were greatly extended during the later middle ages. Anti-semitic rioting was widespread in Germany after the Black Death; it spread from Paris to other French cities in 1380 with the accession of a new king; most seriously of all, Spain experienced the worst pogrom in its history in 1391, also during an interregnum.

Spanish developments are especially interesting. The break-up of relatively satisfactory relationships between Christians and Jews – unusually advanced here during the high middle ages – was sudden and violent during the century after 1380. The expulsion of the Jews in 1492, imitating a process achieved earlier in England in 1290, and in France in 1394, was the medieval 'final solution', the capstone to a gruesome century of Spanish history. A Dominican saint, Vincent Ferrer, excommunicated Christians for associating with Jews, but deplored forced conversions; his earnest anti-semitic sermons helped provoke the 1391 massacres, and directly inspired the extremely stringent anti-Jewish laws of 1412. In fifteenth-century Spain, converted Jews like the ex-Rabbi Jeronimo de Santa Fé, composed anti-semitic writings; the most important and scurrilous work in this genre was the racist *Fortalitium Fidei contra Judeos* by another *converso*, Alonso de Espina. The earliest Grand Inquisitors of the new institution created in 1478 to deal with converted Jews, including the notorious Torquemada, were also of *converso* origin. The Spanish Inquisition accelerated its persecutions after 1485, when the chief Inquisitor of Aragon was assassinated while praying in Saragossa Cathedral; *el santo martyr* had his miracles and his feast day in sixteenth-century Spain, although Rome canonised him only in 1867. Another sign of growing popular anti-semitism in Spain was the decision to exclude converted Jews from holding office in Toledo (1449), opposed by the Papacy, but gradually accepted by Castilian kings. Finally, just before the expulsion, in 1491 Spain claimed its first ritual murder martyr at La Guarda, near Toledo. (Although no Christian child had been reported missing, and no remains were found where the corpse was reputedly buried, Spaniards built a roadside shrine to this 'boy saint' in 1560 which continues to be patronised.)

The Papacy had gone on record against the ritual murder theory as early as 1247, and continued to do so at irregular intervals until 1759; but the persistent spread of these tales in late medieval Europe bears poignant testimony to the strength of grassroots anti-semitism. So does the progressively sharper anti-Jewishness of the fifteenth-century Passion plays, contrasted with their medieval predecessors. Even in Italy the Papacy's opinions about ritual murder were not shared by popular preachers, most notably St Giovanni Capestrano, who toured Italy and central Europe preaching against all enemies of the faith, and who helped engineer some ritual murder trials in Silesia in 1454 during which several Jews were killed. Another great Franciscan preacher, St Bernardino of Feltre engineered the executions of nine Jews for the ritual murder of Simon of Trent in 1475; despite Papal reluctance, Simon was beatified in 1582, and the Jews of Trent were not formally absolved from this accusation until the 500th anniversary of Simon's death, during Vatican II.[18]

As one might expect, the greatest number of ritual murder accusations and local massacres of Jews occurred in the Holy Roman Empire. From 1336 to 1339, armed peasant bands, called *Armleder*, exterminated over a hundred small Jewish settlements in south Germany. Sporadic outbreaks occurred later, including a massacre at Regensburg, seat of the Imperial Diet in 1519, where the site of the synagogue became a pilgrimage shrine to the *schöne Maria*. In Bavaria the ritual murder theme became the plot of a highly popular Renaissance play, the *Endinger Judenspiel*. But the real specialty of Bavaria and south Germany was a different Jewish 'atrocity', the bleeding Host. A Jesuit scholar counted forty-seven examples of bleeding Host stories attributed to Jews throughout Christendom between 1220 and 1514. With a handful of exceptions (Paris 1290, Brussels 1369, Prague 1398, Segovia 1408) they all occurred in Germany. Moreover, in twenty-two instances these stories were followed by massacres of Jews: all but two of these incidents happened in Germany. Miraculous Hosts, 'holy bloods', can of course be found in many parts of late medieval Europe, but only in Germany was this phenomenon linked to massacres of Jews. There were other causes for such massacres. In Sicily in 1474 hundreds of Jews were slaughtered to the cry of 'Long live the Virgin and death to the Jews!' One of the worst pogroms in western Europe began in a Lisbon convent in 1506, when a proclaimed miracle of a lustrous crucifix was ridiculed by a forcibly converted 'New Christian'. A three-day massacre followed, during which over a thousand Jews died, and after which two Dominicans were strangled and burned for fomenting the troubles.[19] (The same Order staged a different but less tragic pseudo-miracle three years later in Bern.)

If anti-semitism resembled Mariolatry by accelerating during the late middle ages from its earlier beginnings, witchcraft resembled purgatory because it was basically a new creation of late medieval popular religion. Of course, the antecedents of fifteenth-century European witchcraft have been traced back to pre-Christian folk beliefs, and to earlier heresy trials which had led to the creation of Papal Inquisitions during the thirteenth century. But it remains true that erudite clerical beliefs about the Devil's power to do harm and to make pacts with humans fused with popular notions about magical spells and night-riding women only during the later middle ages. Complete witch trials involving harmful magic performed by means of pacts with the Devil scarcely existed before the fifteenth century, but they became common after 1425, coinciding with the increased concern about the subject by both clerics and laymen which culminated in the publication of the *Malleus Maleficarum*, the 'Hammer of Witches', by two Dominicans in 1486. The vast majority of the 500 witch trials preserved from medieval Europe occurred after 1425.[20]

The most successful attempt to distinguish between élite and popular elements within late medieval witchcraft has focused on the records of these trials. Only three dozen of the 500 contain original testimony by witnesses or by plaintiffs charging defamation; all of them stress the element of sorcery, while diabolism is completely absent. Moreover, charges of diabolism were present in a majority of witch trials held in ecclesiastical courts, but in only 11 per cent of the larger group originating in secular courts. Diabolism was present in 27 per cent of court cases written in Latin, but in only 6 per cent of vernacular records. Kieckhefer's demonstration is elegant: the closer one comes to popular beliefs about witchcraft, the less talk about the Devil; the closer one comes to the Church, the greater the Devil's role. In only three instances do both witnesses' testimony and interrogations of accused witches survive. In all three, depositions about sick children or cattle are followed by confessions of attending Sabbats, including orgies with Devils and eating dead children. In other types of cases, lengthy Inquisitorial interrogations show judges gradually breaking down peasant resistance – with and without torture – in order to obtain confessions involving both magical harm to others and dealings with devils.[21]

Ultimately, it is not the discriminations between popular beliefs and clerical opinions, but the interplay between them which matters. When witchcraft became a major concern of European governments during the sixteenth and seventeenth centuries, the agreement between peasants and the élites in Church and state was considerable. The process was never a one-way street. Judges learned from popular beliefs in the formative fifteenth-century phase: theory lagged behind courtroom practice. Later on, ordinary people seem to have absorbed much of the system from their religious teachers in early modern Europe. Only in the eighteenth century, as the learned élite (with clerics in the forefront) reclassified witchcraft as a form of superstition, did this interchange cease.

The best guides to late medieval popular religion, whether Protestant (Moeller), Catholic (Toussaert), or anthropological (Christian), seem to agree about many of its major features. Grassroots piety ran broadly and deeply throughout Christendom, and shared many common features in the various regions explored – in Joan of Arc's France, Erasmus's Low Countries, Luther's Germany, even in Machiavelli's Italy. From the names they gave to newborn babies at baptism to their elaborate posthumous rituals to help souls in purgatory, fifteenth-century Christians observed a common core of religious practices as best they could. The poor were at least as devout as the rich, to judge by their role in religious brotherhoods, or their zeal to acquire indulgences; they were less likely than their betters to put Nordic or classical names on their children.

At the same time, scholars of varying backgrounds tend to agree that fifteenth-century popular religion was deformed in various ways. Even by sixteenth-century standards it was 'superstitious'. Its indulgences were too numerous and too farfetched; it stressed commemorative masses at the expense of old-fashioned charity, as the wills of Avignon demonstrate; its veneration of the Virgin and the Eucharist was too miraculous or even too militaristic, as with the *schöne Maria*. Moreover, late medieval popular religion was intolerant. Popes attempted with indifferent success to restrain its anti-semitic excesses. And it was riddled with fears – fears of purgatory, but also fears of witches.

Pious and devout, but superstitious and intolerant, the various aspects of late medieval Christendom at the local level fit together into a coherent pattern. Much of the essays which follow will deal with continuities rather than changes during the next three centuries. But there was one crucial change within early modern Christendom: namely the start of organised religious instruction through catechisms and regular lessons. A Joan of Arc, who learned the fundamentals of sound doctrine at home rather than through a priest, is inconceivable by 1600. Many important continuities endured after 1500, such as the universal custom of baptism with Christian names, or the required annual communion at Easter (and a few other times each year for Protestants and devout Catholics). Unfortunately, popular intolerance of outsiders also persisted after 1500, and grew to include members of rival Christian confessions as well as of Jews and Moslems. The fear of hell, the fear of witches, the anxieties and insecurities underwent few important changes.

Notes

1 William Christian Jr, *Local Religion in Sixteenth-Century Spain* (Princeton, 1981), 14.

2 Bernd, Moeller, 'Piety in Germany around 1500', in Steven Ozment (ed. and trans.), *The Reformation in Medieval Perspective* (Chicago, 1971), 52.

3 Ibid., 53ff, 57. The Huizinga quote is from *The Waning of the Middle Ages* (New York, 1965), 182.

4 Jacques Toussaert, *Le Sentiment religieux en Flandre à la fin du Moyen Age* (Paris, 1960), 122–95.

5 Ibid., 43, 332–4.

6 Louis Binz, *Vie religieuse et réforme ecclesiastique dans le diocèse de Genève (1378–1450)* (Geneva, 1973), 444–5, 393.

7 Etienne Delaruelle, 'La spiritualité de Jeanne d'Arc', in his *La Piété populaire au Moyen Age* (Turin, 1975), 356–62.

8 Lionel Rothkrug, *Religious Practices and Collective Perceptions: Hidden Homologies in the Renaissance and Reformation* (Waterloo, Ont., 1980), 205–41 *passim*. Finucane (n. 12), 199 quoted.

9 Christian, *Local Religion*, 74, 123ff, Appendix B; Rothkrug, *Religious Practices*, 66–8.

10 Toussaert, 282; Rothkrug, 230–39, 86; Christian, 70–125.

11 A.N. Galpern, *The Religions of the People in Sixteenth-Century Champagne* (Cambridge, Mass., 1976), 54; Jacques Chiffoleau, *La Comptabilité de l'au-délà: les hommes, la mort et la religion dans la région avignonnaise à la fin du moyen age (1320–1480)* (Rome, 1980), 448–53; Christian, 51.

12 Christian, 157; Ronald Finucane, *Miracles and Pilgrims* (London, 1977), 201–2.

13 Willy Andreas, *Deutschland vor der Reformation* (Stuttgart, 1932), 176–8; Conrad Beerli, *Le Peintre-poète Nicolas Manuel et l'evolution sociale de son temps* (Geneva, 1953).

14 Huizinga, 144–6. Among the more important recent works on this theme are Alberto Tenenti, *La Vie et la mort à travers l' art du* xve *siècle* (Paris, 1952) and William Forsyth, *The Entombment of Christ* (Cambridge, Mass., 1970).

15 Chiffoleau (n. 11), 323–56, 423 (quote).

16 Christian, 144; Toussaert, 343–4, 759 n. 16; Chiffoleau, 133. The great work on the topic remains Nikolaus Paulus, *Geschichte des Ablasses, in Mittelatter*, 3 vols (Paderborn., 1922–3).

17 Andreas, 144; Christian, 149–50, 51; Chiffoleau, 268–70, 448–53; Toussaert, 482; Galpern, 52–68, 182–6. Cf. Jeanne Deschamps, *Les Confréries au Moyen Age* (Bordeaux, 1958); and Ronald Weissman, *Ritual Brotherhood in Renaissance Florence* (New York, 1981).

18 A valuable introduction to late medieval anti-semitism can be found in Salo Baron, *A Social and Religious History of the Jews*, 2nd edn, 18 vols (New York, 1952–76), xi, 122–91; see also Joshua Trachtenberg, *The Devil and the Jews* (New Haven, 1943).

19 See P. Browe, 'Die Hostientschädung der Juden im Mittelalter', *Römische Quartalschrift* (1926), 167–98; Rothkrug, 64, 68; Baron, xi, 126; Yosef Yerushalmi, *The Lisbon Massacre of 1506 and the Royal Image in the 'Shebet Yehudah'* (Cincinnati, 1976).

20 See especially Richard Kieckhefer, *European Witch-Trials: Their Foundations in Popular and Learned Culture, 1300–1500* (London, 1976); Norman Cohn, *Europe's Inner Demons* (London, 1975); and J.B. Russell, *Witchcraft in the Middle Ages* (Ithaca, 1972).

21 Kieckhefer, 31–7; Russell, 243; Carlo Ginzburg, 'Stregoneria e pietà populare. Note a proposito di un processo modenese del 1519', *Annali della Scuola normale superiore di Pisa*, 30 (1961), 269–87.

2 ERASTIAN PROTESTANTISM

This is not the place to recount the history of the Protestant Reformation one more time, or to recall its common bases of justification by faith, *sola Scriptura*, the break with Rome and thus with continuous traditions. As many specialists have observed, early Protestantism was a movement on behalf of laymen, largely worked out in vernacular publications and sermons – Erasmus's inability to read Luther in German was symptomatic of the failure of the *philosophia Christi* – and closely connected with the spread of printing. The incredible popularity of Luther can be seen in German publishing statistics: in 1518 only about 150 titles were printed in the Empire, but by 1522–4 there were about 800 per year, over half of them by Luther or his close followers. The original Protestant message has been recently summarised as an attempt to desacralise the clergy by attacking its special prerogatives, from auricular confession to celibacy and canon law; the movement itself has been called the first lay enlightenment.[1]

One can learn much about the goals of a movement by studying its Utopias. Luther himself sketched one in the final section of his greatest pamphlet, the *Address to the Christian Nobility of the German Nation*. Shortly afterwards, a talented follower, Eberlin von Günzberg, composed a more elaborate version in the form of laws and statutes for 'Wolfaria', the land where everything goes well. In this paradise religious holidays have been reduced to twenty per year, plus Sundays; clergy are all local people, locally elected, and married; all mendicant orders and all begging have been abolished; confession before communion has become optional; only one prayer, the Our Father, is permitted; all pictures of saints and all pilgrimages to their shrines have been prohibited; all mourning for the dead is limited to one week, with no commemorative masses; and all people who marry clandestinely are put to death.

Given the state of Christendom in 1521, this programme represents a significant revolution in popular religious values and practices; it also prefigures most of the practical reforms which were attempted throughout Protestant territories, with varying success, during the next century.[2]

Protestantism assumed that the Biblical age of miracles had ended during the centuries of Papal corruption, and would not return. It eliminated the role of the Virgin Mary and the saints as intercessors with God. Luther's attack on indulgences meant the abolition of purgatory, and radical changes in popular attitudes towards death: early Protestants shocked their audiences by denouncing priests who said mortuary masses as 'eaters of the dead', *Totenfresser*. Many other significant practical changes were introduced, such as vernacular liturgies, collective hymn singing by the congregation, and a married clergy. Since neither saints nor priests could work miracles (the latter by transforming bread into flesh during the Elevation), Protestants promoted the layman, equipped with his vernacular Bible, to the centre of religious life as a full and equal participant. The new techniques they proposed for purifying the religious life and practices of ordinary Christians were twofold: first, through obligatory attendance at Sunday sermons, preaching the 'pure Word of God', usually for about an hour and often at an 'uplifting' level slightly above their congregations' theological knowledge: second, by obligatory religious instruction for the young or the ignorant, teaching summaries of the main points of Christian doctrine called catechisms. Wherever Protestants gained control, such changes were put into effect rapidly. Luther himself was composing catechisms in the 1520s, while also writing the first set of Protestant hymns. Since they tried to remove the miraculous elements from Christianity, Protestants had to find techniques approved by the Scriptures for dealing with inexplicable or supernatural occurrences; banishing shrines, they recommended prayer combined with fasting to placate the wrath of God.

Early Protestantism was disruptive. Many of its changes were sudden, and a few were truly dramatic – especially iconoclasm. At Regensburg, a major shrine to the *schöne Maria* had been built in 1519 to commemorate the destruction of a synagogue. Over 200 miracles were recorded there in 1521, and published in 1522 by a printer who also published eight of Luther's treatises (although

Luther had attacked the Regensburg pilgrimages by name). In 1524, some iconoclasm occurred but was halted by municipal authorities. Ultimately, in 1542, Regensburg turned Protestant, the image of the *schöne Maria* was shattered, and her church was renamed. Sometimes iconoclasm was accompanied by new Protestant explanations: when the relics of Geneva were dismantled in 1535, the arm of St Anthony was declared to be the penis of a stag, and the brain of St Peter was described as a pumice stone. In England, some iconoclasm was done under state orders when Thomas Cromwell's Commissioners dismantled the kingdom's monasteries in the late 1530s, but in most English churches this task was carried out over a century later by the soldiers of another Cromwell.[3]

Much of the history of implementing Protestant changes in the world of state churches – the Lutheran principalities and city states of the Empire, the Scandinavian kingdoms, and of course England – was less violent than iconoclasm, though much of it happened almost as slowly as the two-step destruction of English images. There was much resistance from, and many compromises with, the old system. Consider the evidence from the English city of York, capital of the northern region which had responded to Thomas Cromwell's dissolution of the monasteries with popular revolts. Here a study of wills illustrates the slow pace of innovation (measured in this instance by the presence of either traditional formulae about the Virgin and the saints, or of clearly Protestant phrases about the merits of Christ alone, in the preambles which disposed of the testator's soul):

Table 2.1 *Wills in Tudor York, 1538–1600*

Period (ruler)	Catholic	Neutral	Protestant	Total
1538–46 (Henry VIII)	163	7	0	170
1547–53 (Edward VI)	88	37	12	137
1553–58 (Mary)	115	14	1	130
1558–70 (Elizabeth I)	56	56	34	146
1571–80 (Elizabeth I)	16	74	56	146
1591–00 (Elizabeth I)	0	92	75	167

Among the gentry of rural Yorkshire the pace of religious change was far more rapid. Between 1540 and 1550 a majority of wills shifted from Catholic to Protestant phraseology, at the moment when official Protestantism was rapidly accelerated after Henry VIII's death in 1547.[4]

The evidence is much the same everywhere. Educated élites accepted the Reformation most rapidly, and the peasantry swallowed it very slowly. An extreme example comes from the north German duchy of Pomerania, which had been Lutheran for several generations, when an official visitation queried its peasantry: the principal farmer stepped forth and announced, 'I believe in the Virgin Mary, the Mother of God, and Jesus Christ her Son,' whereupon everyone else merely remarked, 'I believe what Hans Hille believes'.[75]

In a state-church system, where Protestant leaders insisted on retaining the parish system and on maintaining their obedience to a legitimate secular ruler, such a vast array of changes could not be made quickly. Within the wide spheres of Lutheranism or Anglicanism, it is highly instructive to observe the flash-points of popular resistance to innovations, and to weigh the compromises between new imperatives and old customs worked out in the *modus vivendi* between the state-church and popular religion. In states which were overwhelmingly rural and massively illiterate, how far could a 'lay enlightenment' be implemented?

At its outermost limits, Protestant superstition was slightly more extreme than the most enlightened Catholicism: if Cardinal Bellarmine questioned the efficacy of bells as a preservative against thunder, Lutheran German peasants nevertheless occasionally forced their pastors to ring the bells against storms, especially in places where buildings had been destroyed the first time they were silent.[6] But in general one can establish a spectrum of popular religious practices in which Lutheranism ended many Catholic customs. Anglicanism ended many Lutheran practices, and Reformed Churches tried to go beyond both of them. At the most conservative end of this continuum stand the hundreds of regulatory codes for German Lutheran territorial churches during the second half of the sixteenth century. Combing through them for remnants of Catholic practices, E.W. Zeeden found an impressive number.[7] Most Catholic sacraments were performed in substantially the same way as before, although they were no longer considered as sacraments. Lutheran preachers were required to hear parishioners' confessions before communion, and even keep a register of major sins admitted, although of course no penances could be imposed. Many masses remained in Latin, especially on holy days. Many Catholic holidays were retained (about twenty out of thirty) in most parts of the Empire. The insides of churches were not greatly altered by Lutherans: high altars, crucifixes, organs, stained-glass windows, even special vestments for masses persisted into the eighteenth century. In some places, like Frankfurt on the Oder, pre-Reformation mass books remained in use until the 1580s, and solemn processions were not abolished until 1600. Some points were disputed. Most Lutheran ordinances forbade ringing church bells against storms, but a few permitted it; most required people to make the sign of the cross while praying, but a few prohibited it. Most opposed formal processions, but not all. The formulae of exorcism used at baptisms was forbidden in Prussia in 1558, but re-established a decade later because the nearby Polish Calvinists had labelled them a sign of superstition. Lutheran ordinances seem evenly divided over whether or not to elevate the Host at mass, since the implications of consubstantiation were ambiguous.

In the Anglican 'middle path', the thorniest practical problems were different. The Church of England did not follow the Lutheran policy that every Catholic practice which was not a specific abuse could be kept, nor did it accept the Reformed (and Puritan) principle that everything not specifically recommended by Scripture was superflous and probably superstitious. Accordingly, the Church of England went much further than the Lutherans in cutting back the number of holidays. It changed earlier from Latin to the vernacular, even under Henry VIII, who promulgated not only the English Bible of 1539, but also the English processional liturgy of 1545 which quietly abolished invocations of the saints. It quickly abandoned crucifixes and making the sign of the cross; by 1550 it had prohibited celebrations of patron saints' days by guilds and by parish churches, moving all the latter celebrations to the first Sunday in October. One by one processions ceased, until only one was left: the annual perambulation of parish boundaries in Ascension Week, which was to be done without banners or priestly surplice, yet was still derided by Puritans as 'charming the fields'. Lutherans kept their altars; but most English parish churches converted theirs to communion tables during the sixteenth century, although many English cathedrals retained their altars until the Puritan rebellion of the 1640s. Similarly, such decorations as stained-glass windows or organs generally survived longer in Anglican cathedrals than in parish churches. Anglican clergy were forbidden in 1604 'upon any pretence whatsoever, whether of possession or obsession, by fasting and prayer, to cast out any devil or devils, under pain of the imputation of imposture . . . and deposition from the ministry.' On rare occasions Anglicans seemed more conservative than Lutherans or even Catholics; they had the longest list of canonically-prohibited times for weddings until the eighteenth century (although these prohibitions were not actually enforced). In the vast majority of practical business, the Church of England fully deserves its reputation as middle-of-the-road Protestantism, adopting more radical solutions to concrete questions of worship and religious custom than the Lutherans, yet remaining vulnerable to Reformed criticism that it retained too many superstitious vestiges of Rome.[8]

With respect to black magic, the Erastian Protestant Church traditions are closely comparable. Attitudes towards witchcraft throughout Lutheran Scandinavia were fairly close to those in England. For that matter, the larger Lutheran principalities in the Empire shared important features with Scandinavia or even with England. Whether Lutheran or Anglican, northern state Protestantism was generally less severe in punishing witchcraft than is often believed. English records, chiefly the Essex Assizes so carefully examined by Alan Macfarlane, show an execution rate of under 30 per cent for about 300 people indicted on such charges between 1560 and 1680. This is slightly higher than the 25 per cent rate for Norway between 1560 and 1710, where about 700 were tried for witchcraft. The most extensive prosecutions for witchcraft in Scandinavia occurred in Denmark, with about 2000 trials and a death rate under 50 per cent during the sixteenth and seventeenth centuries. In Sweden, an early flurry of trials in 1590–1614 produced only about 10 per cent of death sentences in 225 cases; but a major panic from 1668 until 1676 eventually resulted in over 200 executions from more than a thousand accusations, often made by children. In the eastern Baltic, there was an early flurry of trials in Estonia, principally of werewolves, and late spillovers from the Swedish panic in the Finnish province of Ostrobothnia, but neither was particularly severe: in the latter instance, there was a 14 per cent execution rate in about 200 trials between 1665 and 1684. Two important general conclusions emerge from this miscellaneous evidence. First, nowhere in northern Protestantism were even half of all arrested witches put to death. Second, much of the most severe witch-hunting took place around or after the second half of the seventeenth century: England's only important panic occurred in 1645, Sweden's a generation later.[9]

There are two important reasons for these shared histories. First, the witchcraft of England and Scandinavia long remained archaic by continental standards. Almost everywhere the root of accusations continued to lay in *maleficia*, the concrete harm done to people or animals, rather than in the witch's dealings with the Devil. The first known traces of a witches' sabbath in any English trial date from 1612, and subsequent references to such assemblies are 'sporadic and inconclusive', according to Keith Thomas. English witches were accused of sexual intercourse with the Devil only during the Essex panic of 1645, while the only reference to an English witch riding on a broomstick occurred in 1663. Scandinavian evidence suggests that these lands were almost as archaic as England. At the Finnish trials of the 1670s, almost 80 per cent of the defendants were charged primarily with *maleficium*, rather than diabolism. Throughout the Swedish panic, apart from one climactic and bloodthirsty year (1675), the courts made consistent and persistent efforts to execute only 'notorious' witches, who had long been feared for harming man and beast. Nowhere in northern Protestantism, not even in Denmark, were arrests and indictments permitted on the basis of testimony from other accused witches. 'There must be a valid case and six witnesses, or a personal spoken confession, before anyone is condemned to death,' ruled a Stockholm court in 1593 with typical caution. Another reason for the peculiarities of English and Scandinavian witch-hunting is the rarity of torture in such trials. Under English common law torture was forbidden except for treason, and Sweden followed the same rules. After 1547 Denmark decreed that 'no person shall be interrogated under torture before he is sentenced'. Such principles were not followed strictly on all occasions: Matthew Hopkins' associates devised ingenious torture-substitutes in 1645, while Swedish officials could use it discreetly and with royal permission in witchcraft cases until 1620. But overall the Anglo-Scandinavian legal tradition compares quite favourably with the Holy Roman Empire or even France in this respect. Little use of torture and no use of accusations by convicted witches meant fewer death sentences for witchcraft.[10]

The Lutheran territories of the Empire have a far blacker record on witchcraft. However, most of the Lutheran states covering northern Germany (with the important exception of the Duchy of Mecklenburg) seem to have held many fewer witch trials than the central or south German lands. In the city of Bremen, for example, only ten of the sixty-two people tried for witchcraft between 1503 and 1711 were tortured; *maleficia* stood firmly at the centre of all accusations; only two Sabbats were described, never involving more than six people; and nobody was executed for this crime after 1603, although the last known use of torture occurred in 1640. Bremen was unusual because its archbishop forbade the swimming of accused witches in 1603, and because the first German translation of Spee's famous warning about legal abuses in witch trials, the *Cautio Criminalis*, was published here. Remarkably, none of its half dozen seventeenth-century cases of demonic possession (two of which involved pacts and sexual intercourse with the Devil) ever led to a witch trial. There were few mass panics in north German Lutheranism, in contrast to the middle Rhine districts or the smaller territories of south-western Germany. Even in southern Germany, the largest Lutheran principality had a tightly-controlled witch-hunting pattern centred on *maleficium*. The Duchy of Württemberg held over 400 such trials, none of which developed into a significant panic. Like Sweden, the witch-hunts peaked relatively late here; Württemberg's worst decade was the 1660s, and the closest thing to a panic occurred in 1683–4.[11]

Harmless magic was a very different matter. Practitioners of 'white witchcraft', those who either diagnosed witchcraft or cured it by therapeutic magic, were numerous throughout early modern Europe. In England, 'cunning folk' of both sexes were reputedly almost as numerous as the parish clergy: 'Out of question, they be innumerable which receive help by going to the cunning man,' lamented an Essex pastor turned pamphleteer. Such people, unlike black witches, were tried in English church courts, where their treatment was remarkably lenient. In the diocesan court at York only one white witch in ten was even forced to do public penance, while about half the charges against them were simply dismissed. Because Lutherans possessed no precise equivalents to England's church courts, the activities of Scandinavian or German 'cunning folk' remain mysterious. At Bremen, local synods were still condemning magical exorcisms of worms in the 1670s, and legislated against magical amulets in the eighteenth century. In Sweden a prominent female magic healer was tried twice by local courts as late as the 1730s, but finally went free. Overall, the treatment of non-harmful magic by Erastian Protestantism seems less rigorous than the punishments meted out to their Mediterranean counterparts by the Spanish or Roman Inquisitions.[12]

There was no Protestant doctrine of witchcraft to help explain the peculiarities of witch-hunting in Protestant countries, although nearly all Protestant writers insisted on a few common elements. Perhaps the most important connecting thread was their emphasis on the extent of divine providence and omnipotence: God is ultimately responsible for permitting evil as well as for doing good, and His ways are 'past finding out'. To Protestant spokesmen, the Devil should not be given blame for supernatural calamities such as hailstorms or inexplicable illnesses. The wonders performed by the Devil were all illusions, *mira* rather than *miracula*. The most perceptive statement by an important Reformer about witchcraft came from the Lutheran theologian Johann Brenz, in an exchange of letters with the great sceptical Protestant physician, Johann Weyer. In his *De Praestigiis Daemonum* (1563), Weyer had praised Brenz for his enlightened views about hailstorms, which had deterred the peasants of Württemberg from blaming witches for damaging their crops. He went on, in an open letter, to ask Brenz to declare himself against the death penalty for witches, who were incapable of performing the evil they claimed to do. But Brenz, while praising Weyer's general approach, disagreed about the correct punishment for witches:[13]

I insist now as before that it is not within the ability of the Devil himself or of any man to cause the disturbance of the elements. It is in God's power alone. Yet I do not doubt that the Imperial law only uses the language of the common man and simply expresses the opinion which magicians and witches also have regarding themselves. For they are persuaded by the Devil that they can disturb the elements with their arts. To this I can hear your response that in this case the law is punishing only an intention and a false persuasion. But this is not so, for the law 'regards the completed and certain attempt as equivalent to the crime itself'. . . . Here the law is right in punishing the 'completed attempt'.

Considering that all mainstream Protestants believed in original sin, almost any Protestant cleric would expect that depraved humanity would attempt to perform harmful magic with or without the Devil's help, if they had the opportunity. Brenz's answer to Weyer explains why no Protestant clergyman ever opposed the death penalty for witches, although most emphatically denied that the Devil could turn men into wolves or cause hailstorms: moreover, witchcraft had a firm scriptural base in Exodus 22:18. Typically, Protestant authors attempted to deprecate the methods of witch-hunting while accepting the reality of witchcraft.

England produced the most noteworthy lay Protestant approaches to witchcraft within the state-church tradition. At one end stood Reginald Scot's *Discovery of Witchcraft* (1584), the most fully developed attack on witch-hunting ever published, except for Weyer's. 'Witchcraft is in truth a cousening art,' Scot proclaimed. 'It is incomprehensible to the wise, learned, or faithful, but a probable matter to children, fools, melancholic persons and papists.' His book was burned by the public hangman by order of the next King of England, James I, himself the author of a *Demonology*. At the opposite end, both chronologically and philosophically, stood Joseph Glanvill, Fellow of the Royal Society and scientific Pyrrhonist, who published a series of essays attacking disbelief in witchcraft (which he called 'Sadducism') between 1666 and 1681. He found Scot 'too ridiculous to answer', but none the less borrowed some of his arguments. Glanvill believed that evidence was more valuable than theories; his basic tactic was to gather the most reliable evidence he could about witchcraft and place the burden of disproof on the Sadducees.[14]

Although Protestants hunted witches as extensively as Catholics during the age of confessionalism, they were lenient towards most forms of non-harmful magic. In theory, Protestants could be more severe than Catholics about all forms of magical practices, since they did not have to worry about the element of word-magic in the Catholic doctrine of the mass (where any consecrated priest can perform the miracle of turning bread into the body of Christ simply by pronouncing words correctly). And important

Protestant spokesmen did attack many forms of magic. An influential Lutheran theologian, Caspar Peucer, in a frequently reprinted work on divination (1553) opposed all forms of 'diabolical' divination, reserving his sharpest barbs for Kabbalists and alchemists, but approved such 'natural' forms as divining rods and even astrology. Others went further. The most thoroughgoing assault, including astrology and cometology amongst its targets, came from the same Protestant who gave his name to the theory of state control over the church – Thomas Erastus. He saw all magical effects, whether from learned or illiterate practitioners, as either demonic delusions or else as natural effects imperfectly understood, and tried to demolish the whole array of 'natural' magic from astrology and alchemy down to the crudest folk beliefs. He detected the magico-medical theories of Paracelsus lurking behind nearly all of it. But the persistence of Paracelsianism, not least in highly 'Erastian' England, illustrates the limits of Erastus's influence among his fellow Protestants.[15]

Throughout much of Protestant and Catholic Europe, governments made *de facto* compromises with learned magic during the sixteenth century, while condemning popular or 'superstitious' magic and executing witches for their *maleficia*. The magistrates of still Catholic Amsterdam ordered in 1555 that 'anyone who is ignorant and untaught, who has not been authorised by their qualifications, rank, degree or other title from the liberal arts' be forbidden from 'exercising the aforesaid unsuitable practices of divination and similar foolishness'. Seldom was the social rather than religious respectability of scholarly magic so blatant, but practices were much the same everywhere. Illiterate folk-healers were banished from Calvin's Geneva and from the nearby Catholic free city of Besançon, while the historical Dr Faustus, a contemporary of Luther's, suffered only occasional harassment from either Protestant or Catholic authorities. Like Calvin, Luther thought that astrologers were impious charlatans; but his Wittenberg colleague, Melanchthon, was an enthusiastic defender of astrology, and in his lectures even seemed impressed by some of Faustus's exploits.[16]

Overall, mainstream Protestantism was no more hostile towards astrology than official Catholicism. One of the greatest Counter-Reformation popes, Sixtus v, issued a stringent bull against astrology in 1586. Among other consequences, it obliged the

University of Valencia to suppress its recently created Chair of Astrology; but it was revived after Sixtus's death, then suppressed again in 1593 when its holder became professor of astronomy (it was revived again in 1608 and finally suppressed in 1613). Other Catholic universities taught astrology even longer: Bologna outlasted a second papal bull in 1631, while Salamanca continued its Chair into the eighteenth century. England, home of the Protestant *via media*, was as hospitable to astrologers as Spain. The group of astrological casebooks left by some major London practitioners between the Elizabethan age and the Puritan rebellion are the only documents of their kind known in Europe. In London this profession was popular, lucrative, and unthreatened by ecclesiastical courts; in the 1650s, William Lilly cast horoscopes for over 4400 customers in twenty-seven months, ranging from peers to servant girls and sailors. The cynical Charles II reportedly employed an astrologer to time an important speech before Parliament, and his successor's physician was still casting horoscopes in the 1680s.[17]

Lutheran Germany can boast of no such group of astrological records, although it offered the largest cluster of alchemists to be found anywhere in Christendom. If the last important alchemist in European history was an English Protestant, the hundred alchemical books in Isaac Newton's library were mainly by Germans. It has been argued that the most exotic and important product of German Protestant alchemy was the Rosicrucian movement of the early seventeenth century, an unstable compound of mystical chemistry and religious politics concocted by a Lutheran theologian from Württemberg on behalf of the Calvinist Elector Palatine. Post-Tridentine Catholics produced nothing as exciting; it seems fitting that the major seventeenth-century assault on alchemy was launched by a French monk, Marin Mersenne.[18]

Did this *de facto* toleration for learned magic among Lutherans and Anglicans carry over into attitudes towards nonconformity to the state church? Were the Germans and English generally more tolerant of astrologers and cunning men than of Catholics and sectarians? To some extent, Protestant spokesmen tried to conflate Catholics with magicians. Reginald Scot claimed to see no real differences between magical practices and Catholic rituals. 'They agree in order, words, and matter, differing in no circumstance but that the Papists do it without shame openly, the other do it hugger-mugger secretly. The Papists... look suspiciously on other cousenors, as having gotten the upper hand over them.' Even earlier, the polemics of Edward vi's time transformed the Catholic phrase *Hoc est corpus* into *hocus-pocus*.[19] Such practices were superstitious but not dangerous. The question was, could they be tolerated?

The English-speaking world tends to view Lutheranism as defensively intolerant, while perceiving Anglicanism as the most tolerant form of Protestantism. Lutheran Germany evokes the religious slogan of the Peace of Augsburg, *cuius regio, eius religio*, and the narrow confessionalism of Scandinavia. England evokes the uneasy toleration of Puritans, the bold experiments of Oliver Cromwell, and the Glorious Revolution of 1688, with Locke justifying the legalisation of religious toleration. Yet during the sixteenth and seventeenth centuries Lutheran Germany and the Church of England were not so very far apart in this respect: Lutheran rulers were more accommodating towards religious minorities, and the English less so, then the stereotype pretends. No Lutheran attempt to impose their confession on a previously Catholic subject population ever failed on the scale of Ireland; no Lutheran state ever executed the range of nonconformists that the English suffered through between 1540 and 1590 – hundreds of priests killed under Elizabeth, hundreds of Protestants burned under Mary, handfuls of both Protestants and Papists killed by Henry viii, and a sprinkling of Anabaptists executed by all Tudor monarchs.

Much of the evidence for Lutheran latitudinarianism has been collected from regions which, like England, changed religions several times during the sixteenth century, although genuine coexistence flourished in other parts of the Empire where no confession acquired a political monopoly.[20] Political Lutheranism could not impose itself successfully in places like Baden-Baden, which became Protestant in the 1550s, returned to a Catholic ruler in the 1570s, and then again became Lutheran in the 1590s. In the Palatinate, which changed from Lutheran to Calvinist in 1560, returned to Lutheranism in 1573 and went back to Calvinism in 1580, it was the Reformed faith which had difficulty taking hold. *Cuius regio, eius religio* failed if overlordship was divided between rulers of different faiths, or if local autonomy and privileges were strong. Heidelberg, the capital of the Palatinate, petitioned its

Elector to retain their Calvinist pastor in 1576, and seven years later petitioned a Calvinist Elector to keep their Lutheran minister (the first was refused, the second accepted).

In parts of Germany like Franconia or Silesia, where the confessional jigsaw puzzle was especially intricate, rigid orthodoxy could not be enforced. Anomalies abounded, and hybrids emerged. Parishioners could easily cross frontiers to attend church or celebrate holidays with people of different faiths. Under such circumstances both clergy and laity might become bi-confessional: a Franconian peasant woman took deathbed communion from both Lutheran and Catholic clerics, while in Baden a priest taught from either Luther's or St Peter Canisius's catechism as requested. Scattered across northern Germany were secularised cathedral chapters, where Lutheran deans marched in Catholic processions in order to collect fees, and where Catholic *Domvikars* supervised Lutheran choirs. Few places could match a nunnery near Bielefeld, whose eighteen rooms were divided equally among Catholics, Lutherans and Calvinists, each group in turn electing its Abbess. Few communities had a ceremony like Wetzlar, where until the eighteenth century Lutheran pastors swore their oath to 'uphold the pure and unadulterated Gospel' between the hands of the city's Catholic dean. Protestant-Catholic hybrids proliferated in northwest Germany, not because of rapid confessional changes but because no clear confessionalism ever emerged. In the lands of the Prince-Bishop of Osnabrück, a thirteen-point questionnaire was asked of the oldest villagers, in 1648, about communion in both kinds, married clergy, the number of sacraments, etc., in order to determine whether they had been Lutheran or Catholic in 1624; but the answers were so inconclusive that the peace commissioners charged with stabilising creeds could not decide where they belonged. The nearby Duchy of Cleves boasted the closest thing to pure religious toleration in the Holy Roman Empire. Here, as in Baden, clerics celebrated both Catholic masses and Protestant communions to different congregations in the same church (and were defended to their respective religious superiors by their congregations); other clerics offered mixtures of Catholicism and Protestantism to the same congregation. In remote corners of Prussia, such religiously-mixed services were still being celebrated as late as 1850. In many corners of Germany, therefore, Lutheranism coexisted with Catholicism (and, more rarely, with

Calvinism), despite the attempts of imperial law in 1555 and 1648 to enforce a clear-cut Erastianism. *Cuius regio, eius religio* was an ideal which was compromised whenever sufficient tensions developed between ruler and ruled.

This same statement applies to England also. The national Church, headed by the sovereign, evolved into a unique style of Protestantism, a *via media* between the Lutheran and Reformed traditions. But this middle path did not logically involve any notion of peaceful coexistence with Dissenters. In one perspective, the history of this 'middle way' begins with Henry VIII's simultaneous executions of three sectarians and three Papists in 1540, and ends with Cromwell's parallel massacres of Irish Catholics and Scottish Covenanters over a century later. The Church of England was the most Erastian of all: nowhere else could one lodge appeals from an archbishop's court with a 'High Court of Delegates in Ecclesiastical and Maritime Cases', created in 1566, which mixed clerics with laymen among its judges.[21] Nowhere in Lutheranism was the prince actually styled Head of the Church. But nationalism *per se* is no handmaiden of religious toleration, as the histories of Scandinavia or for that matter of Louis XIV's France demonstrate. Why, then, did the Church of England become known as the most latitudinarian of all major Protestant faiths? And how did England acquire its reputation as a pacesetter of religious toleration in a major country?

There are very solid pieces of evidence to support such claims. First, England was never religiously unified. Pockets of Catholic recusants existed throughout the Tudor and Stuart dynasties. Illegal Protestant congregations existed under Mary, illegal sectarian congregations under Elizabeth, illegal Anglicans under Cromwell. Throughout the Tudor and Stuart periods, *de facto* coexistence was tempered by various parliamentary laws attempting to impose religious uniformity. At no time was the English political nation, gathered in Parliament, favourable to religious liberty – to expect that would be to make them different from all other early modern Europeans. But under the dictatorship of Oliver Cromwell, some remarkable experiments in latitudinarianism were imposed, in an anomalous situation where the ruler's religion actually favoured a widely tolerant Protestantism. Under a legitimate sovereign of a minority religion, James II, toleration proved impossible to enforce over parliamentary opposition. But throughout Tudor and Stuart England, *de facto* religious coexistence, especially between Catholics and Anglicans, was based on the assumption that any religious activities which did not directly threaten national security could be practised privately. As the dean of living Anglican historians of the Reformation has emphasised, England's great Protestant martyrologist was a staunch enemy of all persecution, who tried to save Anabaptists from the stake and advocated widespread toleration even for Catholics, while the great theorist of England's national Church, Richard Hooker, saw it as only one part of Christendom, and freely admitted that men could be saved under Catholic tutelage.[22]

It is also worth remembering that some of the earliest and most impressive experiments in English toleration occurred overseas, in their North American colonies. The real Utopia of religious liberty was Roger Williams' colony of Rhode Island and Providence Plantations, known to its Puritan neighbours as the 'cesspool of all iniquity', but to historians as the site of the oldest synagogue in British America, and as the first colony whose seventeenth-century governing élite was overwhelmingly Quaker. British North America also contained colonies planted by a leading Catholic peer under Charles I, and afterwards by England's most prominent Quaker under James II, both of which included provisions for general religious liberty in their charters (fortunately for their founders' churches, since both Maryland and Pennsylvania were rapidly overrun by mainstream Protestants). Three of America's thirteen mainland colonies were thus founded principally to offer religious liberty to groups who suffered from discrimination in old England.

Another way in which the Anglican *via media* seems to have been unusually accommodating and latitudinarian is shown by the relatively small numbers of parish clergy who were turned out of office during the rapid changes of official religions between 1545 and 1560. The Catholic restoration under Mary tended to deprive beneficed priests who had married: in a rebellious and well-Protestantised region like Essex, over a quarter (88 of 319) of all parishes changed hands, and in the diocese of London about a third were removed: but in the more traditional northern regions, only about a tenth were deprived. The Protestant restoration under Elizabeth was even milder. Even in the north, only about 2 per cent of all priests were deprived, and one prominent recusant lived in Louvain for many years before losing his parish. Such evidence contrasts vividly with evidence from the Palatinate, where about two-thirds of the clergy in its 360 parishes were deprived when it changed from Lutheran to Calvinist in 1564, and almost 90 per cent were removed when it again became Lutheran in 1577. (Another two-thirds were again removed when it again turned Calvinist in 1584.) But even England looked somewhat different in the seventeenth century: there were massive ejections of parish clergy when the Puritans took over in the 1640s, and over a fifth of British parishes (about 1760) changed incumbents at the restoration of Anglicanism in 1660; even the Glorious Revolution and the onset of greater toleration cost at least 400 non-juring parish clergy their posts in the 1690s. A majority of England's vicars weathered any and all changes in state religions between Henry viii and William iii, but many more suffered deprivation during the seventeenth than during the sixteenth century.[23]

Finally, no discussion of the limits to English religious toleration can omit the case of Ireland. Here the British government created an official Protestant Church of Ireland, with four archbishops, eighteen bishops, and a feeble parish infrastructure. In the long run it proved totally ineffective against a parallel Catholic episcopate, named from Rome after 1600, which was illegal but totally dominant outside the English-held Pale. (In today's Ireland about 3 per cent of the population adhere to the 'national' church.) A minority religious establishment produced a viciously ineffective set of penal regulations against Irish Catholics. The Book of Common Prayer imposed on Ireland by Elizabeth i was in Latin rather than English or Irish – a colonial arrangement which denied the basic Protestant principle of a vernacular liturgy. English Protestantism never tried to evangelise the Irish, being content to exile (1666) or execute (1681) the island's Catholic archbishops. In Ireland, as in North America, religious toleration decreased significantly after the passage of the Toleration Act of 1689. Here the new laws forbade Catholics to sit in the Irish Parliament (1693), or if they were Protestants but with Catholic wives (1697), and ultimately forbade them the right to vote in Irish elections (1727).[24]

From the vantage point of eighteenth-century France, Voltaire saw England as the happy home of religious toleration, a place which had finally decided that 'peace with thirty religions is better than war with none'. He knew England (but not Ireland) at first hand. The English record on religious coexistence does indeed compare quite favourably with Voltaire's France, or even with most of Lutheran Europe – but it seems feeble in comparison with their closest Protestant neighbours, the United Netherlands. Here Jews had settled a half century before Cromwell invited them to England; here Anabaptists and Antitrinitarians had been living undisturbed for fifty years before the English stopped executing them in 1612. Here was a different type of mainstream Protestantism, to which we now turn.

Notes

1 Steven Ozment, *The Reformation in the Cities* (New Haven, 1975), 165. For the printing statistics, see A.G. Dickens, *The German Nation and Martin Luther* (London, 1974), 113–14, and Richard Crofts, 'Books, Reform and the Reformation', *Archiv für Reformationsgeschichte* 71 (1980), 27.

2 Ozment, 97–108; S.G. Bell, 'Johann Eberlin von Günzberg's Wolfaria – The First Protestant Utopia', *Church History*, 36 (1967), 122–39.

3 Bernd Moeller, *Imperial Cities and the Reformation* (Philadelphia, 1972), 58–60; R.M. Kingdon, 'Was the Protestant Reformation a Revolution? The Case of Geneva', in Kingdon (ed.), *Transition and Revolution* (Minneapolis, 1974), 85; Ronald Finucane, *Miracles and Pilgrims* (London, 1977), 202–3.

4 Table adapted from D.M. Palliser, *Tudor York* (Oxford, 1979), 249–54; compare A.G. Dickens, *The English Reformation* (London, 1964), 192; and Margaret Spufford, *Contrasting Communities* (Cambridge, 1971), 320–44.

5 Boguslav von Chemnitz (1605–79), quoted in E.W. Zeeden, *Die Entstehung der Konfessionen* (Munich-Vienna, 1965), 89.

6 Owen Chadwick, *The Reformation* (Harmondsworth, 1964), 430; Keith Thomas, *Religion and the Decline of Magic* (London, 1971), 70–1.

7 Ernst W. Zeeden, *Katholische Uberlieferungen in der Lutherische Kirchenordnungen des 16. Jahrhunderts* (Münster, 1959), summarised in his *Entstehung der Koniessionen*, 81–94.

8 Thomas, 62–6, 482–6, 620; Chadwick, 407; Palliser, *York*, 116; Jasper Ridley, *Thomas Cranmer* (Oxford, 1962), 247; also much valuable detail in A.L. Rowse, *The England of Elizabeth* (London, 1950), ch. 10.

9   Cf. Alan Macfarlane, *Witchcraft in Tudor and Stuart England* (London, 1970), 57–63; Bengt Ankerloo, *Trolldomsprocesserne i Sverige* (Lund, 1971), 324–39 (English summary); Antero Heikkinen, *Paholaisen Littolaiset* (Helsinki, 1969), 374–94 (English summary); and H.C. Erik Midelfort, 'Heartland of the Witch-Craze: Cethral and Northern Europe', *History Today*, 31 (February 1981), 31.

10 Ankerloo, 327; Macfarlane, 139–40; Thomas, 439–49; Heikkinen, 386.

11 Herbert Schwarzwälder, 'Die Geschichte des Zauber- und Hexenglaubens in Bremen', *Bremisches Jahrbuch*, 46 (1959), 156–233; 47 (1961), 99–142; H.C. Erik Midelfort, *Witch-Hunting in Southwestern Germany 1562–1684* (Stanford, 1972), 77–80, 158–63; Gerhard Schormann, *Hexenprozesse in Nordwestdeutschland* (Hildesheim, 1977), includes a few exceptions to this generalisation.

12 Macfarlane, 115–34; Philip Tyler, 'The Church Courts at York and Witchcraft Prosecutions 1567–1640', *Northern History*, 4 (1969), 84–110. Compare Carl-M. Edsman, *A Swedish Female Folk Healer from the Beginning of the 18th Century* (Uppsala, 1967).

13 Erik Midelfort, 'Were There Really Witches?', in Kingdon (ed.), *Transition and Revolution*, 225.

14 Reginald Scot, *The Discovery of Witchraft*, Williamson (ed.), (Carbondale, Ill., 1964), Book xvi, ch. 2; Wallace Notestein, *A History of Witchcraft in England, 1558–1718* (Washington, 1911), 285–93; Moody Prior, 'Joseph Glanvill, Witchcraft, and Seventeenth-century Science', *Modern Philology*, 30 (1932), 167–93.

15 Lynn Thorndike, *A History of Magic and Experimental Science*, 8 vols (New York, 1923–58), vi, 493–501 (Peucer); v, 652–71 (Erastus); D.P. Walker, *Spiritual and Demonic Magic from Ficino to Campanella* (London, 1958), 156–67; Alan Debus, *The English Paracelsians* (Chicago, 1965).

16 Thorndike, v, 378–405 (Melanchthon); Willem Frijhoff, 'Prophétie et société dans les Provinces-Unies aux xviie et xviiie siècles', in *Prophètes et sorciers dans les Pays-Bas xvie-xviiie siècle* (Paris, 1978), 276; Frank Baron, *Doctor Faustus: From History to Legend* (Munich, 1978); William Monter, *Witchcraft in France and Switzerland* (Ithaca, 1976), 170.

17 Thorndike, v, 247–51; vi, 145–78; Ricardo García Cárcel, *Herejía y sociedad en al siglo xvi: La Inquisicíon en Valencia 1530–1609* (Barcelona, 1980), 255–7; Thomas, 304–21, 355.

18 Frances Yates, *The Rosicrucian Enlightenment* (London, 1972); B.J.T. Dobbs, *The Foundations of Newton's Alchemy* (Cambridge, 1975), 49–53.

19 Scot, *Discovery*, Book xv, ch. 22; Maurice Powicke, *The Reformation in England* (Oxford, 1941), 91.

20 See Zeeden, *Entstehung der Konfessionen*, 68–80, for substance of next two paragraphs.
21 Powicke, 136.
22 Dickens, 323–4.
23 *Ibid.*, 245; Rowse, 440; Christopher Hill, *The Century of Revolution 1603–1714* (London, 1961), 242; David Ogg, *England in the Reigns of James* II *and William* III, 2nd edn. (Oxford, 1963), 233; B. Vogler, *Le Clergé protestant rhénan au siècle de la Réforme, 1555–1619* (Paris, 1976), 310–12.
24 Ogg, 8–9; Margaret MacCurtain, *Tudor and Stuart Ireland* (Dublin, 1972), 118, 167–71, 175, 189.

Bibliographical Note

For excellent introductions to some of the main issues which underlie this section, see Gerald Strauss, 'Success and Failure in the German Reformation', *Past and Present*, 67 (1975), 30–63; and Jean Delumeau, 'Les réformateurs et la superstition', *Actes du Colloque L'Amiral de, Coligny et Son Temps* (Paris, 1974), 451–87.

3 THE REFORMED TRADITION

What chiefly distinguishes Calvinism from Lutheran or Anglican Protestantism? Not the latter's emphasis on state control of the Church, although in fact such control was carried furthest in England and the Lutheran countries. The man who gave his name to the sixteenth-century form of Caesaropapism, Thomas Erastus, was in fact a Swiss Calvinist who worked mainly in the Palatinate, Germany's most important Reformed territory. It could be argued that Calvinism in the Palatinate and throughout the Empire differed from the Reformed tradition elsewhere in Europe, where it usually demanded considerable autonomy for its Church *vis-à-vis* the secular government. The most important distinction between the Reformed tradition and other major varieties of Protestantism, however, is not its ecclesiology but its emphasis on a more thorough and more strenuous Reformation, to be implemented through a more rigorous discipline.

There was significant friction between the Reformed confessions and other types of magisterial Protestantism. On one side is the shock experienced by Calvinists attending Lutheran services, whether the Swiss theologian Musculus visiting Eisenach in 1536, or the English Puritan ambassador visiting a Swedish cathedral in 1653. On the other side is the enormous volume of pamphlets and legislation by German Lutherans directed against the bogeyman of Calvinism, which in hundreds of instances was portrayed as worse than Catholicism, and the equally massive amount of Anglican literature opposing Puritanism. Militarily, it was rare for Lutheran and Calvinist states to co-operate, as the Thirty Years War tragically demonstrated: in England, the military conflict between Episcopalian and Puritan was overt. Nowhere did Protestantism function as a diplomatic or military bloc, despite the seriousness of the Counter-Reformation.

Yet almost everywhere the Calvinists were the most militant anti-Catholics. Calvinist strenuousness inspired a radical approach to virtually every aspect of liturgy and worship for which clear Biblical precedents could not be found. Hence the Reformed tradition removed all organs and stained-glass windows from their churches as relics of idolatry. (Lutherans kept their organs, and eventually employed them to play magnificent chorales by the late seventeenth century.) Calvinists wished to abolish all holy days except Sundays, but also to honour Sundays in ways (said their enemies) akin to those used by Jews on Saturdays. Calvinist opposition to religious art was deeper and more systematic than that of other major types of Protestants, which explains some of the controversies between them. Calvinism stood more firmly against all forms of customary 'superstitions'. It seems significant that Calvin, unlike Luther, took the trouble to compose pamphlets against the cult of relics (1543) and against astrology (1549), two different, but to him equally scandalous, practices. Calvin's most important populariser, Pierre Viret, carried on this attack against idolatry and superstition in dozens of treatises which focused on ceremonies or institutions rather than dogma.

Viret's best known and most successful efforts were polemical dialogues directed against a variety of Catholic practices. Many of his topics were staples of Protestant controversialists since Luther, but Viret was distinctive because he tried to find pagan origins for each and every Catholic practice he ridiculed, and important because he was popular. Viret was unusual because his satires generally avoided *ad hominem* attacks and licentiousness, although he was capable of crudeness, being the first Protestant to claim in print that the doctrine of transubstantiation implied cannibalism : his worst failing was sheer prolixity. His dialogues attacked such topics as Catholic prayers, especially the Ave Maria; the use of chaplets; the cult of saints; the Catholic view of Church councils; "true and false ministers;" the institution of the Papacy; and monastic vows. He composed a cycle of twenty dialogues against Catholic funeral practices, embellished with such titles as 'The Alchemy of Purgatory', 'The Adolescence of the Mass', and 'Papal Necromancy'. His most ambitious satire was *Le Monde à l'Empire ou le monde demoniacle* (1561), whose title punningly stressed how things were getting worse (*empirant*) in a world infested by demons.[1]

If we examine how far and how quickly the Reformed tradition was actually implemented in Calvin's city of Geneva or in Viret's land, the neighbouring Pays de Vaud, we find remarkable differences depending upon whether the environment was urban or rural. At Geneva old customs, whether Catholic or merely non-Christian, were uprooted relatively quickly. Within a decade of Calvin's return in 1541, for instance, Geneva forbade parents to give non-Biblical names to their children, thus eliminating both saints' names and traditional local names like Balthasar or Besançon. Nonconformists of various kinds were denounced to, and examined by, the new institution called the Consistory, composed of both laymen and clergy. Calvin had few illusions about Geneva's inhabitants or how his version of godly discipline needed to be applied: 'We must have rough halters for rough donkeys,' he reportedly remarked. Unacceptable practices were punished by excommunication and, where necessary, handed over to secular authorities as criminal defendants. House-by-house tests of doctrine, carried out annually in the 1550s, unearthed some closet Catholics, but many more cases of religious ignorance. Thanks to an unusual set of records, we can see the machinery of Consistory excommunications at work around the time of Calvin's death in 1564. In the city, about 15 per cent (73 of 472) of those excommunicated during the final three years of Calvin's life were accused of religious ignorance; only a dozen were punished for 'idolatry', i.e. Catholicism, and only three for 'superstition', including one man who was handed over to secular authorities to be burned as a witch. A much larger sample shortly after Calvin's death, in 1567–9, showed only about 1 per cent excommunicated for ignorance, while 'idolatry' and 'superstition' combined added up to 3 per cent. However, the pattern of excommunications for the rural districts around Geneva showed a significantly different pattern. Here nobody was excommunicated for either ignorance or Catholicism, but 15 per cent (78 of 530) were excommunicated for superstition, mostly for consulting magical healers or *devins*. Such magicians were rarely found in Geneva itself; only three or four *devineresses* turned up in her seventeenth- and eighteenth-century court records. In general, magical superstitions were not an important problem in the Republic of Geneva after Calvin's death, except of course for maleficient witchcraft.[2]

In Viret's Vaud the Reformed tradition took a great deal longer to root in. A full century after the introduction of Protestantism, its records still bristle with a variety of traditional practices long since condemned as superstitious. Between 1630 and 1670 there were multiple complaints about people venerating a sacred tree trunk which reputedly cured gout; about a sacred fountain which supposedly cured people of 'evil spirits' (pilgrims arriving by boat prostrated themselves on the shore and made other 'superstitious gestures'); about parishioners crossing into Catholic territory to attend local festivals and dances; about ringing church bells at times of threatening weather; or about observing traditional holidays like 'St Bridle's Day', when no horses were supposed to work. A century after Viret's attacks on Catholic funeral customs, the pastors of Vaud still denounced their parishioners for distributing alms upon leaving the cemetery; no fewer than eight times between 1635 and 1690 they denounced them for making long speeches at burials – a custom suspiciously close to Catholic prayers for the dead. A century after Viret's patient search for the pagan origins of Catholic customs, the pastors of Vaud were still fighting against some purely pagan superstitions like May Day, or the spicy 'furry soup' given to bedded-down newlyweds by nocturnal intruders.[3]

The Reformed clergy of Vaud had a few superstitions of their own. In 1645, an assistant pastor was suspended for performing exorcisms: he had treated his patients like any other folk healer, feeding them soups fortified with herbs and red wine, applying a piece of paper covered with crosses to their heads while chanting prayers in Latin, and sending them to drink from Vaud's sacred fountain. Around 1700, another Vaud pastor routinely noted the astrological signs under which the babies in his baptismal register were born. All these ministers routinely celebrated a ritual peculiar to Reformed Protestantism, but popular mainly in its rural districts – the day of community fasting and prayer. These were *ad hoc* Reformed holy days, observed even more strictly than Sundays, decreed in order to ward off God's wrath for some particular calamity; they resemble Catholic penitential processions, because in both instances the gesture of collective appeasement operated in an external, mechanical fashion. Such collective fasts were not a product of the early Reformation, but developed during the later sixteenth century. They were decreed in Vaud for such things as the assassination of Henri IV, the massacre of Valtelline

Protestants, earthquakes (1621, 1639), and even for the passage of a comet in 1665. By the 1650s an annual fast day was decreed throughout Protestant Switzerland, to be celebrated on some weekday in September; but by 1678 the clergy of Geneva complained that Vaud and Switzerland had too many fast days, arguing that it had become a habit rather than a stimulus to genuine repentance and reform.[4]

Vaud was full of magical healers, like other Protestant and Catholic regions. Comprehensive codes condemning all forms of white magic, specifying stiff fines for first offenders and banishment for repeaters, were read from every pulpit in Vaud in 1599, 1610 and 1640. But the *devins* were difficult to dislodge. Lausanne's pastors complained to their government about a notorious white witch on at least four occasions between 1650 and 1665 before anything was done. In the Alpine area of Vaud, magical healers continued undisturbed into the nineteenth century.

The most dangerous aspect of magic, witchcraft, was treated very differently in urban Geneva than in rural Vaud. The latter province probably holds the dubious distinction of being the most witch-ridden corner of Protestant Europe. Pastor François Perreaud, who published a *Démonologie ou Traité des Demons et Sorciers* in 1653, complained in his preface that he had been attacked by French Catholics 'because of the quantity of witches whom they say are burned ... particularly in the Pays de Vaud, inferring from that that our religion was the cause of it'. He used the example of Job to show that the righteous always confront the worst difficulties, but he did not try to disprove the basic accusation. The best evidence suggests more than 2000 witch trials in Vaud, a province of about 160 parishes, between the Reformation and 1680, and local samples suggest an execution rate of 90 per cent, far greater than in other parts of French Switzerland. The single worst panic in Switzerland, when twenty-seven witches were burned within four months, occurred in Vaud, at Chillon. Occasionally, the authorities tried to slow down Vaud's witch-hunts, for instance by decreeing stricter rules for searching out the Devil's mark, in 1652; but the medical historian who studied the issue proved that these reforms were not followed. A more effective route may have been a new catechism, imposed by the government in 1666, which deliberately played down local obsessions and fears about witchcraft. Its final Article stressed that even if a child had been marked by the Devil, he must not lose confidence in his ultimate salvation.

If Vaud had the worst record on witchcraft in Protestant Europe, its neighbour, Geneva had one of the best. Apart from special types of panics (in 1530 – before the Reformation, 1545, 1568–9, 1571, and 1615) when scores of people were accused of spreading plague with magical grease, the Republic of Geneva executed only sixty-eight witches in 318 trials, a lower conviction rate (21 per cent) than even the English county of Essex. After 1626, only one accused witch was executed at Geneva, and she was condemned only after surgeons had been imported from Vaud to verify her Devil's mark when Genevan surgeons refused to do so unequivocally.[5]

Urban Geneva and rural Vaud thus had vastly different campaigns against diabolical witchcraft, as against more innocuous superstitions. But in both places the Reformed Church enjoyed a complete religious monopoly; no other religions were tolerated, until Louis xiv compelled the Genevans to let his ambassador hold private masses in the 1670s, and long before the Lutherans were granted a church in Geneva in 1707. In both Vaud and Geneva the Reformed Church arrived in the 1530s, immediately succeeding late medieval Catholicism. Nowhere else in Europe did such conditions obtain. Either the Reformed Church was the first serious Protestant movement but failed to control secular government, as in France or Poland-Lithuania; or else it controlled secular government, but came as a second-wave Protestant movement, following Lutheranism in the Empire or Anabaptism in the Netherlands. Nowhere outside Switzerland, except perhaps in Scotland, could Reformed Churches maintain a durable monopoly on early modern popular religion – but in Scotland it arrived relatively late, and never truly controlled a large part of the country, the Highlands.

In Erastian Germany two of the four secular Electorates turned Calvinist, the Palatinate in 1559 and Brandenburg in 1613. Although a few small principalities followed suit, Calvinism never became a truly serious threat to the overwhelmingly Lutheran tone of Protestant Germany. Because it arrived late, its grasp on popular religious practice was never complete. In Brandenburg, where Lutheranism had taken root for two generations, Calvinism never became a majority creed except among the governing élite;

in the Palatinate, where it arrived earlier, it was interrupted by a Lutheran interval lasting seven years, by a much longer Catholic occupation in the 1620s, and, most damagingly of all, by a converted Catholic Elector, Johann Wilhelm (1690–1716), whose persecutions drove thousands of Palatine Calvinists to America and drew rebukes from the Catholic Emperor Joseph I. Throughout the Empire, the Reformed Church lacked the element of relative autonomy from secular authority which seems an important part of this tradition almost everywhere else. At best, German Calvinism produced an excellent catechism, which was exported to the Netherlands Reformed Church, but it seems little more than a parenthesis in the popular religious life of the Empire.

The first Calvinist Elector-Palatine was a remarkably pious prince with an unusual record towards superstition and toleration. Frederick III was the first important Protestant ruler to flatly prohibit witch trials in his domains, but he was also the first to arrest his ecclesiastical superintendant for antitrinitarianism (he escaped, fled to Transylvania, and eventually converted to Islam in Istanbul; one of the three ministers arrested with him was executed in 1573). Frederick III removed most of the incumbent Lutheran pastors in his lands, but given the confessional checkerboard in the Rhineland, such changes were more often nuisances than catastrophes: when the neighbouring Duchy of Zweibrücken turned Reformed in 1588, twenty-seven of its sixty-three Lutheran ministers were discharged, but nineteen of them found new posts only 12–30 miles away from their original parishes (five retired and two moved farther away).[6]

The history of the Reformed Church in Calvin's native France is the story of a well-organised system with congregational Consistories and regional synods to enforce discipline, which never managed to gain control of the state, not even when the legal heir to the French throne belonged to their confession (1589–93). French Calvinists had a legal existence in two distinct periods: a generation of religious warfare (1562–98), punctuated by phases of *de facto* toleration; and a longer phase of *de jure* toleration under the Edict of Nantes (1598–1685), punctuated by a return to religious warfare in the 1620s. Its history thus has two distinct phases, corresponding to the militant and military circumstances of the sixteenth century, and to its place as a tolerated minority during the seventeenth century. At its zenith, in the 1560s,

Reformed spokesmen claimed that a sizeable share of the French nobility favoured them, while churches sprang up like mushrooms throughout the kingdom. But religious warfare took its toll. By 1598 France was only about 10 per cent Huguenot – a share which gradually shrank to about 5 per cent by the time their legal toleration was revoked in 1685.

In the sixteenth century, the French Reformed Church tended to flaunt its differences from the surrounding Catholics. Huguenots prided themselves on their austerity and their discipline, on living more sober and upright lives than their neighbours; even their new church buildings, like the temple at Lyons in 1567, were daringly simple and plain. They sang Psalms at work or play, or even before going into battle; they ostentatiously avoided ostentation by such changes as abolishing all funeral ceremonies. Perhaps the supreme example of sixteenth-century Reformed behaviour (and its limitations) was the military code adopted for their armies in 1562. Where the king's army was forbidden to play cards, they forbade all games of chance; where the king's code regulated duels, they forbade them; where the king prohibited his troops from pillaging churches, they prohibited all pillaging. A Huguenot officer later recalled that their troops maintained this ideal discipline for two whole months. Seldom did the Huguenots aim so high or fail so quickly.[7]

Because France was the only major western European state with two legal Churches, the history of the French Reformed Church under the Edict of Nantes deserves attention. Its seventeenth-century keynote was *détente*. In villages whose population was wholly or predominantly Huguenot, legal toleration meant autonomy. A Dapuhiné village church evoked by Daniel Ligou seems typical of such cases. It grew slowly as late as the 1660s. Its consistory found few people to excommunicate, but held interminable discussions about seating order in pews (the seventeenth century was the golden age of preoccupation with precedence; at no other time would a layman attempt to organise the history of his parish around pew seats). Its membership still gave Biblical names .o their children, although a few noblemen were named Caesar, Alexander or Olympia. Its clergy struggled with some success to keep funerals rudimentary, but with less success to prevent intermarriage with Catholics. Over half a century this church decreed only four special fast days, because there were few local emergencies to preoccupy them. Other places where Huguenots formed about half the population lived almost as quietly. One such, at the edge of the Pyrenees, shared not only its municipal offices, but also its local church between the two congregations. When Catholic clerics refused to allow the names of Protestant officials to be put on a new church bell alongside their Catholic counterparts, the village erased the Catholic names also, and composed a dignified rebuke in their minutes: 'Only the ignorant are unaware that the garments and authority of Protestant officials have the same colour and the same extent as the Catholics.'[8]

Perhaps most interesting of all were the rare spots where the Huguenots formed a majority within a major city and its hinterland, most notably the diocese and city of Nîmes in Languedoc. After Richelieu captured La Rochelle in 1628, Nîmes was the only important French city with a Protestant majority (in 1663 it had 12,000 Huguenots and 8000 Catholics, while the diocese of Nîmes contained 76,000 Protestants and 34,000 Catholics). Until forbidden to do so by an edict of Louis xiv in 1681, Catholics converted to the Reformed Church of Nîmes in greater numbers than Huguenots converted to Catholicism: several monks, an ex-Rabbi turned Catholic, even a parish priest who converted in front of his scandalised congregation at Easter mass, joined their ranks. From top to bottom, Nîmes saw much intermarriage between confessions: the city's most zealous Catholic diarist had to remarry a Huguenot widow in order to raise enough money to make his daughter a nun. Coexistence took many other forms. As late as 1673, the Consistory censured several prominent members who had attended the funeral sermon preached by a Jesuit for the city's ardent Counter-Reformation bishop; ten years later, a cathedral canon sheltered a fugitive Huguenot minister from royal soldiers for many weeks and arranged his escape. Nîmes' institution of higher learning was peacefully divided between Huguenot professors and Jesuits, just as the city's four consuls were evenly split.

If the ruling classes of Nîmes shared irenic attitudes, its lower classes shared some of the same superstitions. The Consistory had to deal with Huguenots who went on pilgrimages or attended masses in order to cure their sick children. In 1670, a Protestant notary and an innkeeper were censured for using a *devin* and subsequently beating a man whom they accused of witchcraft. In

1675 the local synod opposed the practice of summoning pastors at all hours to administer baptism to dangerously ill babies, a practice 'superstitious and contrary to the Word of God'. Nîmes' Consistory fulminated against the 'superstition and vanity' of employing paid mourners in 1609, but eight years later they allowed a nobleman's widow to erect a tombstone. Such developments resemble those in the Palatinate, surrounded by Catholic and Lutheran neighbours, whose consistories struggled against mixed marriages and more sporadically against Catholic or pagan superstitions; for that matter, they seem similar to developments in the solidly Reformed Pays de Vaud around 1650. One important difference was that, because they never controlled regional governments, French Calvinists were unable to carry on witch trials. For the same reason, they were powerless to resist their legal disestablishment in 1685. But they avoided assimilation into Catholic France and maintained much of their difference even in the more relaxed seventeenth century: 'I cannot help but observe, to the shame of Catholics', wrote a Jansenist priest in 1680, 'that dancing is prohibited with much rigour by the discipline of the so-called Reformed churches of France.'[9]

In only two other places did the Reformed tradition successfully establish itself: Scotland and the United Netherlands. It became the official state creed, unlike France, but maintained some autonomy from secular authority, unlike Germany. Yet in other vital respects Scottish and Dutch Calvinism were remarkably different. In the former land, it succeeded a pre-Tridentine Catholicism in a relatively remote and rustic environment. In the latter, it came long after Lutherans and Anabaptists had made inroads in the most urbanised and commercially-advanced region of northern Europe. Culturally, it is a very long way from the land of Macbeth to the first bourgeois nation of Europe, from a Reformed Church whose Kirk sessions were controlled by feudal lairds, to one whose Consistories were staffed by urban patricians. In Scotland much of the governable territory was safely Calvinist by the early seventeenth century; but in the Netherlands, which was conquering and trying to assimilate heavily Catholic territories in the early 1600s, the Reformed Church never succeeded in becoming a majority faith. The juxtaposition of Scotland's rusticity and clear ascendance of the national Reformed Kirk after 1580, with the urbane sophistication and ineradicable religious pluralism of the United Netherlands after it officially proclaimed the Reformed faith at the same time, obviously provides more differences than similarities.

Nowhere were the differences between Reformed Scotland and the Reformed Netherlands more total and more complete than in their respective attitudes towards witchcraft. Scotland was one of the most heavily affected parts of Protestant Europe, while the Dutch became the first European nation to abandon witch-hunting entirely. The situation in Scotland was less dreadful than in Vaud, or in the most witch-ridden parts of Lutheran Germany like Mecklenburg. Considering that Scotland was the only place where serious witch-hunting was inaugurated by a monarch who believed himself personally threatened by witchcraft and had even published a *Demonology* in 1597, its record is not overly bleak. Because witchcraft was the only crime besides treason which required recourse to the Scottish appellate court, they executed fewer than half of all accused witches whose cases were actually tried there (other witches were tried locally under special licences granted by the High Court of Justiciary, and few of them were acquitted). Our most plausible estimate is that Scotland executed about 1350 witches in 2300 trials between 1560 and 1700 – statistics resembling most closely those from the kingdom of Denmark. It seems pertinent that Scottish witch trials began in earnest after James I married a Danish princess; witch-hunts were started simultaneously at Edinburgh and Copenhagen in order to explain the misfortunes of various royal voyages sent to fetch her to Scotland. Still, it cannot be denied that Scotland's witch-hunts were the worst anywhere in Reformed Europe outside Vaud, and that the national religion played a role in them: the most thorough recent investigation of this subject concluded by echoing W.E.H. Lecky's judgement of 1841 that 'Scotch witchcraft was but the result of Scotch Puritanism.' Here witch-hunting coincided chronologically with a strenuous attempt to impose a godly society. Nearly two-thirds of Scotland's known witches were tried between 1639 and 1670, while the Covenanting movement was at its peak.[10]

In contrast to Lecky stand the observations of Johann Huizinga that

however much we may prize Calvinism as a factor in our civilisation, it is undeniable that Dutch intellectual life in the seventeenth century, seen as a whole, was but partially rooted in the doctrines promulgated at

Dordrecht. In this connection we must mention a fact that, in my opinion, cannot be stressed enough... namely that we gave up the atrocities of witch-hunting more than a century earlier than our neighbours.[11]

The last certain execution of a witch in the Netherlands occurred at Utrecht in 1591; the last known witch trial occurred in the province of Holland in 1610, ending in an acquittal. A famous Dutch moralist, and devout Calvinist, Jacob Cats earned his legal spurs in that case. It was true that most Dutch *predikants*, like other Protestant clergy, continued to believe in the reality of witchcraft and were even able to defrock one of their colleagues in 1692 after he had published a voluminous attack on the basic concept of witchcraft; but it is also significant that the Dutch Reformed Church, frequently able to influence the devout and orthodox House of Orange, never attempted to stir up witch trials after 1610. The Netherlands stands at one extreme of the European spectrum with respect to witch trials: nowhere else did they end so rapidly and so quietly.

The Netherlands also stands at the extreme point of European governments with respect to *de facto* religious toleration during the sixteenth and seventeenth centuries. In the land which gave birth both to Erasmus and to the leader of the Münster Anabaptists, Jan of Leiden, the values of the former clearly prevailed. Considering the size and duration of the Anabaptist movement in the northern Netherlands – it was strong enough to mount a serious *coup* against the largest city in the north, Amsterdam, in 1535 – it is remarkable that no heretics were condemned to death in the province of Holland after 1553, and very few in Friesland after 1557. Local magistrates refused to co-operate with Inquisitors, just as they would soon fail to enforce laws against *maleficium*. The consequences of their attitudes were that a middle-sized Dutch city like Rotterdam contained no fewer than ten different religious groups in the seventeenth century. Sephardic Jews migrated here when their havens in the Catholic Low Countries were no longer safe; Antitrinitarians came here when Poland and Transylvania were no longer reliable asylums. In the seventeenth-century Netherlands the physical safety of any religious group – even of those who belonged to none at all – was assured, on condition that they did not openly proselytize: that privilege was reserved for the official Dutch Reformed Church. It is true, as Huizinga stresses, that many of the greatest geniuses in seventeenth-century Holland did not belong to it: Grotius was a Remonstrant (and long an exile for essentially religious reasons); Rembrandt was a Mennonite; the poet, Vondel, was Catholic; Spinoza was a Jew expelled from the synagogue. But one could also list many prominent seventeenth-century Dutchmen who belonged to the Reformed Church. The important point is that one did not have to convert to it in order to enjoy a satisfactory career.[12]

The United Netherlands was not perfectly tolerant in the 1600s. What persecution – perhaps harassment is more adequate – there was tended to be directed towards the largest and most dangerous unofficial religion, Catholicism. Members of the old faith were certainly a majority, probably a large majority, of the population in the time of William of Orange. When it was suggested in 1587 that only one-tenth of the population adhered to the Reformed Church, its *predikants* did not dispute the estimate. Under such circumstances, the leaders of the rebellion against Spain felt a need to discriminate against Philip II's religion. In 1580 the province of Utrecht outlawed Catholic services; the next year Holland followed suit, and added some censorship of religious and political works 'which at the present time might lead the unlearned... common man to error, disruption, and sedition'. At the height of repression, after the triumph of militant predestinarianism at the Synod of Dordrecht (1619), Roman Catholics were forbidden to worship in public or in private. Netherlanders could not own Catholic books or religious objects, sing Catholic hymns, or celebrate Catholic holidays. No Catholic could hold any official civilian or military post. Harassment extended to the point of denying Catholics the right to send their children abroad for an education, and to denying unmarried Catholic women the right to make a will. What made freedom of conscience possible for Dutch Catholics during the century and a half that these penal laws remained in force was the simple fact that they were rarely enforced with any rigour. Despite them a few known Catholics became magistrates, and many more became army officers. After 1630, camouflaged Catholic churches and meeting-places were created in all major towns; everyone, including the local *predikant*, knew what and where they were, but could not destroy them or even prevent camouflaged Catholic priests from serving them. A vivid illustration of the religious climate in seventeenth-century

Amsterdam is provided by the contrast between the snug synagogue and the larger Catholic church known as Our Lord of the Hayloft (*Ons Lieve Heer op Solder*), created by knocking out the third-floor walls between three adjoining merchants' houses. Unlike England, Holland executed no Jesuits; there were few around, because the local clandestine Catholic hierarchy disliked them, being Jansenist. In the long run, harassment had some effect. If the Netherlands were overwhelmingly Catholic in the 1580s, they were much less so by 1650, when Protestants comprised half the population. (By 1795, when the Dutch Reformed Church lost its official status, Catholics formed about 40 per cent of the population.)[13]

Unlike the Netherlands, Scotland has no reputation as a paragon of religious toleration. It was, after all, the Scottish Parliament which in 1645 solemnly addressed the English Parliament 'against the toleration of the sects and against liberty of conscience'. Yet one can make a case for relatively benign persecutions here. Scotland's most distinguished Reformation historian has pointed out that, unlike England, Scotland carried out its religious changes without dissolving its monasteries, and without provoking any popular rebellions against Protestant innovations. Saying mass was a capital crime, but only one priest was ever martyred for this reason. However, the seventeenth century was less tolerant than the sixteenth: it was Scottish Covenanters who massacred Catholic prisoners and civilians to the cry of 'Jesus and no quarter!', and who denounced toleration as 'wicked' when they came to power. Moreover, Scotland's changes of official religion in the second half of the seventeenth century seem to have been even more disruptive than in England; about 30 per cent of her thousand parishes changed hands at the Episcopalian restoration in 1660, while fully half of her parish clergy were replaced when Presbyterianism became the established creed after the Glorious Revolution.[14]

In Scotland, the history of the Reformed Kirk's battle against vestiges of pagan and Catholic superstitions resembled that in Vaud; the Highlands, which spoke a different language and maintained a nomadic way of life, preserved more bizarre practices than even the Swiss Alps. As late as 1656, the supposedly Protestant residents of the north-west coast worshipped St Mourie with sacrifices of bulls, adorations of stones, libations of milk, and other pagan practices. But in the Lowlands the Reformed Kirk,

backed by state support and untroubled by any Catholic neighbours, usually managed to enforce its legislation as well as the
Swiss. The Kirk of Scotland had bishops between 1567 and 1692
(except at the Covenanting period between 1639 and 1662) who
could sometimes overrule the decisions of parish Kirk sessions; it
was possible, for instance, for the Session to force men to do
public penance for failing to work on Christmas Day, while the
Archbishop of St Andrews could imprison a man for *not* observing
Christmas a few years later.

Public fasts were as common here as in Vaud; the Covenanters
forbade everything the Swiss did, and surpassed them in the
matter of observing Sundays. Even before the Reformation (and
before the Council of Trent) a Scottish archbishop proposed
stringent laws against profaning the Sabbath, as well as opposing
dancing and May Day celebrations; afterwards the Calvinist state
forbade all work, recreation, and drinking on Sundays (1579) with
the ministers adding a ban on Sunday travel. These laws remained
on the books until the twentieth century, although they were no
longer enforced by secular penalties after 1700. At the zenith of
Scottish Sabbatarianism in the 1650s, children were punished for
playing on Sundays, and their parents for carrying water, sweeping
their houses, or taking out ashes on Sundays. If there was a
superstitious excess within the Reformed Kirk of Scotland, here is
the place to seek it, especially among the secessionist Covenanters
who formed the Reformed Presbyterian Church and the four
Presbyterian breakaways of the eighteenth century who ultimately
formed themselves into that very Scottish institution, the United
Secessionist Church, in 1820: the latter continued to lament the
prohibition of witch trials, and practised a stern type of kirk-stool
discipline long abandoned by the official Kirk.[15]

Given the religious pluralism and high literacy of the
Netherlands, signs of overtly superstitious behaviour are difficult
to come by. The more extreme cases were likely to be practised by
foreigners, like the thousands of seasonal migrant workers from
Catholic Westphalia who still, in the early twentieth century, knelt
in front of a dockside garbage dump which had once been the site
of a medieval pilgrimage chapel, patronised by their ancestors
since the fifteenth century, but demolished by Protestants soon
after 1600. The Reformed *predikants* were much less successful
than their Scottish on French counterparts in persuading their

flocks to give up such pastimes as theatricals or dancing. In outlying rural provinces they had some success in persuading people to observe a strict Sunday and to ignore 'Popish' holidays like Christmas or New Year's Eve; but even at the height of their power in the 1620s they could not close down the theatres or dance-halls in Holland's cities. Similarly, Dutch Calvinism was unable to abolish the *kermis*, the local patron saint holidays which, by the seventeenth century, had stretched into two- and three-week Breughelian carnivals that were perhaps the wildest orgies staged anywhere in Protestant Europe.[16]

The range of collective behaviour within the different national strands of the Reformed tradition was thus quite wide, from Dutch *kermis* to Scottish fast days and Sabbaths. Yet these two Churches share a significant similarity, which has acquired considerable importance in recent decades. Both Scotland and the Netherlands sent out settler colonies during the first half of the seventeenth century (the age of Dordrecht and the Covenant), largely from rural areas. Nowhere – certainly not in these two cases – did the Reformed colonists attempt to proselytise or otherwise assimilate the surrounding peoples. The Calvinist concept of the Elect meshes poorly with the missionary or the assimilationist impulse. Largely for such reasons, the heirs of the Ulster and Cape Town plantations, the transplanted Scots Presbyterian and the Dutch Reformed *Boer*, continue to uphold the principles of exclusiveness, on religious and ethnic grounds. In few places is the Reformed tradition stronger today than in Northern Ireland or South Africa; and nowhere have the uglier consequences of its élitism been more apparent. In its home countries, the Reformed tradition has coexisted with, and even welcomed, modernity throughout Europe: the orderly, neat, hard-working, self-confident Calvinist had been something of a commonplace even before Max Weber drew attention to him: its members have been disproportionately important in modern France, they have contributed to the remarkable prosperity of Switzerland, they have tempered the English, and perhaps even more the American, character. Calling attention to Calvinism's share in the colonial intolerance of Ireland and Africa does not argue against the reality of the European or American experience, but merely points to the other side of the coin.

Notes

1 Henri Vuilleumier, *Histoire de l'Église réformée du Pays de Vaud sous le régime bernois*, 4 vols (Lausanne, 1928–32), I, 503–49; for a fuller account, Jean Barnaud, *Pierre Viret, sa vie et son oeuvre (1511–1571)* (Saint-Amans, 1911).

2 Archives d'Etat, Geneva, Registres du Consistoire, Annexes 3–5, partially summarised in E.W. Monter, 'The Consistory of Geneva, 1559–1569', *Bibliothèque d'Humanisme et Renaissance*, 38 (1976), 477–81; also W. Deonna, 'Superstitions à Genève aux XVIIe et XVIIIe siècles', *Archives Suisses des traditons populaires*, 43 (1946), 343–90.

3 Vuilleumier, II, 228–34, 632–6.

4 Ibid., 188, 620–5, 632–4, 636–42; Olivier Fatio, 'Le jeûne genèvois', *Bulletin de la société d'histoire et d'archéologie de Genève*, 14 (1971), 397–435. The part of Reformed Europe which most closely resembled Vaud with respect to fast days was seventeenth-century Scotland.

5 E.W. Monter, *Witchcraft in France and Switzerland* (Ithaca, 1976), 105 n.25, 108, 163–4, 49–50, 54–5.

6 See Bernard Vogler, *Vie religieuse en pays rhénan dans la seconde moitié du XVIe siècle* (thesis, Lille, 1974); and his book, *Le Clergé protestant rhénan au siècle de la Réforme, 1559–1619* (Paris, 1976), 310–14; E.M. Wibur, *A History of Unitarianism*, 2 vols (Boston, 1945–52), I, 258–64.

7 See Janine Garrisson-Estèbe, *Protestants du Midi, 1559–1598* (Toulouse, 1980), for an overview; Alain Dufour, *I a Guerre de 1589–1593* (Geneva, 1958), 25, on the military code.

8 D. Ligou, *Le Protestantisme en France de 1598 à 1715* (Paris, 1968), 135–8; J.-F. Soulet, *Traditions et réformes religieuses dans les Pyrenées centrales au XVIIe siècle* (Pau, 1974), 300.

9 Robert Sauzet, *Contre-réforme et réforme catholique en Bas-Languedoc: Le diocèse de Nîmes au XVIIe siècle* (Paris, 1979), 165–184, 255–74, 398–404, 409–9.; J.-B. Thiers, *Traité des divertissements* (1680), quoted in Y.-M. Bercé, *Fête et révolte* (Paris, 1976), 150.

10 Christina Larner, *Enemies of God: The Witch-Hunt in Scotland* (London, 1981), esp. 63, 83, 202, 61, 91.

11 J. Huizinga, *Dutch Civilization in the Seventeenth Century* (London-Glasgow, 1968), 59.

12 Based on Geoffrey Parker, *The Dutch Revolt* (London, 1977), 62, 151–5, 202–4, 260.

13 L.-J. Rogier and P. Brachin, *Histoire du Catholicisme hollandais depuis le XVIe siècle* (Paris, 1974), 9–72, 249–53; a good overview is in C.R.

Boxer, *The Dutch Seaborne Empire 1600–1800* (London, 1965), 123–6.

14 Gordon Donaldson, *Scotland: Church and Nation through Sixteen Centuries*, 2nd edn (Edinburgh, 1972), 65, 85–6, 93 and n.

15 Ibid., 65, and ch. 8; also T.C. Smout, *A History of the Scottish People 1560–1830* (London, 1969), ch. 3, esp. 71–2, 78–80.

16 Willem Frijhoff, 'Prophétie et société dans les Provinces-Unies aux xviie et xviiie siècles', in *Prophetes et sorciers dans les Pays-Bas xvie–xviiie siècle* (Paris, 1978), 278; Paul Zumthor, *Daily Life in Rembrandt's Holland* (London, 1962), 188–92.

Bibliographic Note

A useful introduction to some of the central issues of this essay is the article by J. Estèbe and B. Vogler, 'La genèse d'une société protestante: étude comparée de quelques registres languedociens et palatins vers 1600', *Annales*, 31 (1976), 362–88.

4 THE MEDITERRANEAN INQUISITIONS

Ever since the development of canon law in the twelfth century, Christendom had been filled with various kinds of ecclesiastical tribunals. In only one part of Europe, however, were such tribunals truly important during the early modern era. Mediterranean Catholicism boasted three major Inquisitions – Spain, Rome, Portugal – which like their medieval predecessors had been created in order to extirpate heresy. But during the sixteenth and seventeenth centuries these Inquisitions acquired jurisdiction over many other issues, and their records were filled with interrogations and trials of people accused of various erroneous beliefs falling well short of formal heresy; of a wide variety of morals offenders; of magicians, both harmful and harmless; of owners and readers of prohibited books; and many other things. On a map of social controls in early modern Europe, Mediterranean Catholicism offers a distinctive profile. It was the only part of Christendom where crimes like witchcraft or bigamy were often tried in church courts rather than secular courts: north of the Alps and Pyrenees, even Catholic states kept such crimes firmly under lay jurisdiction. Some of the most important and most profound differences between Mediterranean and northern Europe in the early modern centuries can be traced to the extraordinary range of both religious and morals controls vested in these peculiar institutions.

According to a tenacious but unexamined legend, the Inquisitions of Mediterranean Europe were bigoted and bloodthirsty, with the Spaniards as the cruellest of all. Their very names have long been bywords for intolerance. Yet when historians finally began to explore the huge bulk of Inquisitorial records systematically, quite different results emerged, and a new consensus has begun to take shape. Two principal findings now seem to be established, although the results are still incomplete. First, these

61

Mediterranean Inquisitions were less bloodthirsty than Europe's secular courts in the early modern era. Between 1550 and 1800, they put nearly 150,000 people on trial, but sentenced only about 3000 to death: most major secular courts had higher ratios during the sixteenth and seventeenth centuries. The second major new development is that the Mediterranean Inquisitions, unlike the secular courts, seemed more interested in understanding the motives of the accused than in establishing the facts of his crime. Inquisitors, who carefully preserved the anonymity of their informers, have always appeared less careful of the rights of the accused than secular courts. But current research suggests that Inquisitors were more psychologically astute than the secular judges, better able to make accurate – and frequently lenient – judgements. On the whole, they were far less likely than secular judges to rely on torture in order to convince themselves of the truth of a suspect's statements. Because they tried to look into men's minds rather than to establish legal responsibility for a crime, Inquisitorial cross-examinations read very differently from those of secular tribunals, and offer far richer material to historians of customs and beliefs.

The Inquisitions of Mediterranean Europe resembled a triptych. In the central panel is the Spanish Inquisition, the oldest, largest, and most famous of the three. Vast as the Spanish empire and more centralised than most other parts of that empire, it included twenty regional tribunals at its peak, stretching from Sicily and Sardinia in the east, to Mexico, Lima and Cartagena in the Americas. Thanks to a competent central bureaucracy which insisted on detailed annual reports from each of its far-flung branches and minutely supervised their most serious cases, it has been the easiest for social historians to study.[1] From 1550 until the end of Spain's Habsburg dynasty in 1700, we possess tabulations on over 50,000 cases handled by its various branches. Less than half of them were true heresy trials against Judaisers, *Moriscos*, Protestants or mystical *alumbrados*. The majority are a variegated bouquet of incorrect beliefs (*proposiciones hereticos*), of *supersticiones*, of lascivious priests trying to seduce their penitents in the confessional, of blasphemers, bigamists, and assorted morals offences including (in the Kingdom of Aragon only) sodomy. Overall, their chronology and typology looks as follows:

Table 4.1 *Spanish Inquisition cases, 1550–1700*

Total cases by period			Total major crimes (%)	
1540– 59:	4182	(209/yr)	*Moriscos*	11,311 (23)
1560–1614:	29,584	(538/yr)	Judaisers	5007 (10)
1615– 39:	7561	(302/yr)	Protestants	3499 (7)
1640– 99:	7765	(127/yr)	*Proposiciones*	14,139 (29)
			Supersticion	3750 (8)
			Sex crimes	4031 (8)

Chronologically, the peak decade for the Spanish Inquisition occurred from 1585 to 1594; its workload slackened visibly after 1615 and more sharply after 1640. The balance between heresy and other kinds of offences also varied enormously in different periods, and also among different tribunals during the same period. Each tribunal had its own distinctive inquisitorial profile, for instance, the senior tribunal of Castile, Toledo, pursued *Moriscos* in only 13 per cent of its cases during the peak phase (1560–1614), while the senior tribunal of Aragon, Saragossa, devoted a majority of its attention (56 per cent) to them. From 1615 until 1700, Toledo was preoccupied with Judaisers, who formed 44 per cent of its cases, while they accounted for only 3 per cent at Saragossa. (*Moriscos* now accounted for only 2 per cent of inquisitorial business at both tribunals.) Among non-heretical crimes, *superstición* accounted for only 1 per cent at both these tribunals before 1615, but afterwards rose to 12 per cent of Toledo's business and 21 per cent of Saragossa's.[2] Such comparisons could be extended indefinitely.

The Spanish Inquisition was the most famous of these institutions, and has now become the easiest to analyse quantitatively. We cannot yet see so clearly into the side panels of this triptych – the Portuguese and Roman Inquisitions – but it seems reasonably certain that the smaller Portugese system, which included only three European and one overseas branch, and covered a far smaller population than Spain's, was relatively more active and more bloodthirsty than its Iberian sister after 1550. Although the massive records in Lisbon's archives contain no series of annual reports, estimates from its *autos da fé* indicate that during the quarter-millenium after its establishment in 1540, the Portuguese

Inquisition tried over 30,000 people and executed more than Spain. Portugal's high levels of activity and executions were due to her relatively large *converso* population, most of whom had immigrated shortly after their expulsion from Spain in 1492, and had been forcebly baptised a few years later. (These poorly-assimilated 'New Christians' have preserved aspects of their Jewishness into the present century in Portugal's most remote region.)[3]

The Roman Inquisition, created in 1542 to cover the Italian peninsula, differed from the Iberian models in two important ways. First, it did not ordinary publically humiliate its convicted offenders in front of huge crowds at *autos da fé*, but attended to much of its business in relative privacy. Second, the Roman Inquisition remained separate from Italy's secular governments, except of course in the Papal states. Unlike the Iberian peninsula, in Italy relations between the inquisition and the state were latent with possible frictions. Different accommodations were worked out in different regions. The most unusual occurred in the lands of the anti-Papal, although orthodox, Venetian Republic, where lay representatives sat alongside the Inquisitors at all official sessions. It is difficult to generalise about the Roman Inquisition for other reasons. Although it possessed a supervisory board in the form of a standing committee of the College of Cardinals, this institution did not leave well-organised central records like the Spanish or even the Portuguese. Because of Jacobin destruction in the 1790s and Napoleonic looting afterwards, most of the records of both the central and local apparatus of the Roman Inquisition have been dispersed.[4] However, some evidence has survived, enough to permit at least tentative comparisons with Spain. Annual caseloads per tribunal seem rélatively comparable in Italy and in Spain; because Italy was much more populous than Spain and Spanish America combined, the Roman Inquisition probably handled at least 50,000 cases between 1550 and 1750. Differences between Rome and Spain seem qualitative rather than quantitative: Italian tribunals as far apart as Venice and Naples pursued different types of heretics from the Spaniards, and concentrated on different kinds of non-heretical offences.

The Spanish Inquisition had been organised in 1478, near the end of a process of Jewish conversion dating back to the great pogroms of the 1390s, while the other two were much younger, with Portugal only acquiring a permanent, ongoing institution between 1540 (first full-scale *auto da fé*) and 1547 (durable re-establishment of the system) and Rome created in between. Spain's Inquisition pre-dates the expulsion of the Jews, while the other two were contemporaneous with early Protestantism. But all three shared some similar patterns of activities during their long histories, chiefly at their beginning and ending. The most elaborate model of long-term Inquisitorial activity has been constructed by J.-P. Dedieu, based on the important and extremely well-preserved records of the Spanish tribunal of Toledo. Of course, Toledo is not Spain, let alone Portugal or Italy; but the first and last phases of Dedieu's model seem to apply everywhere in Spain. The first phase was a massive and lethal hunt for insincere Jewish *conversos*, which lasted until 1525 or 1530. The final phase, during the eighteenth century, saw a toothless, 'enlightened' Inquisition, mainly pursuing old-Christian miscreants and undisciplined priests. In between came the phases of the most numerous trials which covered a remarkably wide range of charges. The Portuguese Inquisition, we have suggested, never quite outgrew the first phase of its Spanish cousin, remaining preoccupied with crypto-Jews and their activities up to the time Pombal reduced them to impotence in the 1760s. Consequently, the graph of its activities over time seems different from Spain's, resembling a 250-year oscilloscope with rising and falling curves, and with a very gradual fall-off to somewhat lower levels of activity after 1690. As late as 1720–40, these three Portuguese tribunals were averaging over a hundred cases per year – at least as many as all twenty Spanish tribunals put together.[5]

On the other hand, the fragmentary picture of the Roman Inquisition bears more resemblance to Dedieu's Toledan model, with one crucial difference: here the first phase completely lacked the anti-semitic thrust of the Spaniards or Portuguese, being dominated by a zealous hunt for native Protestants. Even at Naples, where Protestantism was not a serious problem, heretics provided almost half of all cases in the first recorded decade (1564–73) of its operations. In the north, which was afflicted with several varieties of Protestantism including Anabaptism, Holy Office trials of such heretics began sooner, and lasted far longer. Over 80 per cent of Venice's Inquisitorial trials before 1580 were for Lutheranism or related forms of crypto-Protestant behaviour.

In the remote and mountainous north-eastern corner of Italy, the Friuli, well over half of all Holy Office trials before 1595 involved Protestants. A sample of about 130 sentences reported to Rome in 1580–1 from all of northern Italy from Piedmont to the Venetian Republic showed a persistent preoccupation with Protestantism.[6]

However, the various branches of the Roman Holy Office shifted their major focus sometime before 1600, replacing this preoccupation with heretics by an obsession with repressing magical practices and other forms of superstition. In the Friuli, under 10 per cent of the 390 trials before 1595 were for illicit magic, while over the next fifteen years nearly half of its 558 cases fell under this heading. Elsewhere, this shift was less dramatic and occurred sooner; at Naples, illicit magic became the single largest rubric of inquisitorial business in the 1570s, and remained so in every decade until the 1720s: at Venice, the shift from heresy to magic occurred just as abruptly as in the Friuli, but a dozen years earlier. During the seventeenth century, all the magical arts from witchcraft to fortune-telling became the great concern of the Roman Inquisition: in each tribunal about 40 per cent of all cases throughout the century can be labelled as the repression of superstitious magic. Sicily, which belonged to the Spanish rather than the Roman system, provides an interesting comparison: in the seventeenth century it had a lower ratio of trials for *superstición* (25 per cent) than any branch of the Roman system, but a higher percentage than any other European branch of the Spanish system. This concentration on uprooting superstitious magic by the Cardinals of Rome's Congregation of the Holy Office tells us much about the inner dynamics of Counter-Reformation Italy after 1590—especially when we consider that such cases accounted for only a tiny fraction of the business of Portugal's Holy Office, and for not much more than an eighth of Spain's Inquisitorial business at the same time.

If it is sometimes difficult for present-day historians to untangle the various threads in inquisitorial trials of 'Lutherans', it is even more difficult to understand the precise nature of charges labelled by inquisitorial clerks and modern archivists as 'superstitious magic'. However, it is clear that most of these cases were *not* accusations of witchcraft. This crime came within the legal purview of all three Inquisitions, but each of them seems to have investigated such charges with reluctance, and punished the culprits with leniency. The mildness of Inquisitorial judgements on witchcraft contrasts strikingly with the severity of secular judges throughout northern Europe during these centuries, and even with the Inquisitors' own attitudes towards relapsed or obstinate heretics. It is fascinating to observe the Spanish *Suprema* advising its branches as early as 1538 that Inquisitors should not believe everything in the *Malleus Maleficarum*, even if the author 'writes about it as something he himself has seen and investigated, for the cases are of such a nature that he may have been mistaken, as others have been'; or to watch the branch of the Roman Inquisition in the Duchy of Milan confronted with a local panic which filled their prisons with seventeen accused witches in 1580. Nine of them were acquitted of all charges, five more were released under oath, one confessed, and two made partial confessions – but even these three got off with minor penances. Given such attitudes, it is not surprising to learn that only a handful of people (a dozen Basques in 1610, half of whom had already died in prison) were ever executed for this offence by any of the Mediterranean Inquisitions, despite many opportunities to do so. Even the 1610 crisis was only the spill-over from an earlier and more severe panic on the French side of the Pyrenees; and although the cascade of denunciations eventually led to more than a thousand confessions, mostly by children or adolescents, no one was convicted after 1610 because the evidence behind all these charges was meticulously picked apart by a relentless Inquisitor, Alonso Salazar y Frias, who had been partially responsible for the 1610 deaths. It is strange to contemplate the enormous piles of paper accumulated by the Inquisitors about witchcraft, and the very small amount of real human damage resulting from them.[7]

Witchcraft cases involved only a small share of the Holy Office's dealings with superstitious magic. Only in one corner of Italy, the Friuli, can we see relatively clearly what this entire category included, thanks to a relatively precise inventory of Holy Office cases (see Table 4.2).

Over time, proportionately more and more men were charged with illicit magic in the Friuli. By the middle period, men formed a majority of those arrested for all forms of magical superstitions except witchcraft; after 1671, when witchcraft became less frequent, men comprised three-quarters of all 'superstition' defendants. As a modern scholar observed,[8]

Table 4.2 *'Magical arts' and the Friuli Inquisition, 1596–1785*

Offence	1596–1610		1611–1670		1671–1785	
	Men	Women	Men	Women	Men	Women
'Magic' in general	10	16	12	7	18	7
Divination-necromancy	5	6	3	1	4	0
Therapeutic Magic	50	60	39	48	0	2
Benandanti	5	5	26	8	6	0
Love Magic + *Tamiso*	18	26	40	23	44	7
Spells vs. wolves	2	1	7	21	0	0
Spells vs. bullets	0	0	1	0	8	0
Spells to get rich	0	0	0	0	34	1
Other spells	3	8	3	2	8	2
Maleficio- Witchcraft	8	39	12	72	20	29
Total	101	161	143	182	142	48

Many men declared, without difficulty, that they had tried to give their souls to the Devil in exchange for money; but the Devil, although frequently invoked, never appeared, and so they gave up, more from ineffective magic than from respect for the faith. . . . Everything happened among a disillusioned witch, a retiring Devil, and an indifferent Inquisitor.

The world of the Enlightenment had truly arrived.

As we have seen, Mediterranean Inquisitors tried several thousand people for illicit magic, but executed only about a dozen witches. For that matter, they killed relatively few people for heresy during the early modern centuries. Compared with the numbers of Anabaptists slaughtered in Austria, the Empire and the Low Countries, the Mediterranean Inquisitions seem almost gentle – with one crucial exception. During the first phase of the Spanish Inquisition, *conversos* were killed in large numbers; the tribunal of Valencia alone executed no fewer than 754 Judaisers between 1484 and 1530. By contrast, all twenty branches of the Spanish Holy Office combined executed a total of 775 people between 1540 and 1700. A majority of these were still Judaisers, but they also included several dozen *Moriscos*, over a hundred Protestants (most of whom were foreigners, especially Frenchmen), about fifty homosexuals, and a handful of Basque witches. Scattered among 50,000 defendants, they add up to a death rate of 1.6 per cent; Valencia from 1484–1530 had about 2000 cases, virtually all Judaisers, for a death rate of 38 per cent. After 1530, the crime punished with the greatest *relative* severity by the Spanish Inquisition was bestiality, which fell under their jurisdiction only in Aragon: here one finds twenty-three deaths in fifty-eight sentences between 1540 and 1593, for a death rate of 40 per cent. (By contrast, the death rate even for Judaisers was now about 10 per cent.) Of course the Spanish Inquisition continued to punish people after 1530. Thousands of Judaisers, *Moriscos*, bigamists and other miscreants were sent to do 'unpaid penance at the oar' in the king's galleys, while further thousands of men and women were whipped and banished at *autos da fé*, and thousands more were confined to house arrest or to a religious institution for lengthy periods, in addition to their confiscated property, public penances and family humiliation. Still, the central fact remains that relatively few people were put to death after 1530.[9]

Portugal, which never outgrew its *converso* problem, seems more bloodthirsty than her Iberian cousin. According to the most plausible estimate, this Holy Office condemned about 1175 Judaisers to death at 750 *autos da fé* between 1540 and 1760, while anotner 633 were executed in effigy. This works out to an execution rate of almost 4 per cent higher than the overall Spanish ratio after 1550, yet lower than the Spanish execution rate for Judaisers alone between 1550 and 1700. We do not know how many people were executed by the Roman Inquisition because so many of its records have disappeared. But, as the case of Giordano Bruno indicates, we know that the most important defendants were often transferred to Rome itself for final questioning and sentencing. The best estimate of heretics executed at Rome during the first century of the Inquisition's activities hovers around one hundred – mostly Protestants but also a few Jews – with most executions occurring in the 1560s and 1570s, but very few after 1610. We also possess estimates for a few branches of the Roman system. Venice, which sent Bruno to Rome in 1593, executed about fifteen Protestants during the sixteenth century; the smaller branch in the Friuli executed only five. By way of comparison, Sicily (a Spanish tribunal) executed two dozen Protestants, one Jewess, and four *Moriscos* between 1542 and 1615. Since Venice investigated about 800 suspected Protestants before 1600 while Sicily handled fewer than 200 of them before 1615, the ratio of trials to executions seems significantly lower in the Roman than in the Spanish Inquisition. The Roman system probably executed fewer than half as many people as the Spaniards after 1540, or fewer than a third as many as Portugal. We must remember that the Roman Inquisition had no problems with *coversos*, that it was much concerned with uprooting superstitions whose practitioners were never sentenced to death, and that the Protestant movement which originally preoccupied it had ceased to be a serious threat by 1580.[10]

If neither the Spanish nor the Roman Inquisition was especially bloodthirsty during the sixteenth and seventeenth centuries, and if heretics of all varieties amounted to less than half their total business, they none the less managed to busy themselves with a variety of social controls. Some of their business was essentially morals control: bigamy cases, for example, comprised close to 10 per cent of their activity at Naples and Sicily, and more than 5 per cent in Spain. They also passed sentences against priests who had made sexual advances to women in the confessional. Though rare in the sixteenth century, such cases accounted for 5 per cent of Spanish activity after 1615, and over 15 per cent after 1700; Italian figures are similar. However, thought control lay behind most of the Mediterranean Inquisitions' non-heretical investigations, just as it conditioned their approach towards heretics. In the Spanish system, 30 per cent of all cases were *proposiciones heréticos*, which involved ferreting out, correcting, and often re-educating ordinary 'Old Christians' about important errors in religious beliefs surviving from the era before catechising became widespread: errors about the virginity of Mary, about the nature of the Trinity, about the sin of fornication between unmarried people, about the Last Judgement – mistaken opinions about many significant parts of Christian dogma kept Inquisitors in all parts of Spain busy, particularly after the Council of Trent had clarified doctrines and revitalised religious education. Since these Inquisitions' attitudes towards superstition also amounted to a type of thought control rather than punishment for specific deeds, about half of all inquisitorial business in Italy or Spain after 1600 can be reasonably labelled as such.

One of the more important, though not statistically numerous, aspects of Inquisitorial thought-control was censorship of reading. All European governments tried to control the printing and distribution of unorthodox or seditious works, but only the Inquisitions tried to reach the reader as well, and only the Spanish Inquisition offered a streamlined model of repression where the same institution controlled printers, booksellers and readers (the College of Cardinals maintained separate congregations for the Inquisition and the Index). Revising the Index of Prohibited Books was a major task for the Spanish *Suprema*: Cardinal Quiroga spent years on the masterpiece of the genre, the two-volume set of 1583–4. The principles of censorship used by the Spanish and Italian Inquisitions (who were completely separate in this, as well as in other respects) included all works by notorious heretics, all vernacular quotations from the Bible, and nearly all anonymous works in the vernacular; but they also included works of inferior literary merit, many works of chivalry, and all works on magic or anything which advocated illicit love. In other words, the Mediterranean Indices prohibited not only heretical books, but also magical or lascivious books; the literary censorship of their Inquisitions was in defence of morality as well as of orthodoxy. Magical or obscene literature occupied much space in official Indices, and formed a sizeable share of the illegal literature which actually circulated in Mediterranean countries. We still know relatively little about the enforcement of Inquisitorial censorship on the consumers, as opposed to the producers and distributors, of illicit books. This offence seems to have been more frequent in Italy than in Spain, more common in the Venetian Republic than in the *Mezzogiorno*. At Venice, this offence accounted for almost 10 per cent of sixteenth-century Inquisitorial cases, and the defendants included such well-known figures as Giordano Bruno and the Neapolitan philosopher, G.-B. Della Porta, both charged with owning 'prohibited books' in 1592. Those works were basically magical rather than heretical. The Italian Inquisition in the Friuli unleashed a major campaign against illegal books from 1641 to 1660. It unearthed ten 'heretical' titles, including Galileo's *Two*

Dialogues, and one by Paolo Sarpi; but they were outnumbered by twenty-one magical works, including three astrologers, and dwarfed by fifty-nine instances of 'lascivious and obscene' books. At the same time, a noble Spaniard's library destined for public auction in 1651 contained no fewer than 250 volumes which were either prohibited or required expurgations, few of which were heretical. In the long run, censorship should probably be seen as part of the Inquisitors' struggle against superstition and immorality rather than part of the fight against heresy.[11]

Perhaps the most exciting aspect of recent studies on the Mediterranean Inquisitions is not the quantitative distribution of their business over three centuries, but their methods of procedure. By the standards of modern secular justice, Inquisitorial courts were remarkably slow, and remarkably painstaking. If some of their peculiarities, such as the anonymity of accusers, protected informers, many other customs worked in favour of the accused. Because they were primarily concerned less to establish the deeds of heresy, blasphemy, magic or whatever than to understand the *intentions* of the person saying or doing such things, their most serious distinctions had to be made between repentant and unrepentant sinners, between accidental and deliberate sinners, between knaves and fools. Unlike most early modern secular criminal courts, Inquisitors placed little faith in torture as a means to extract truth from difficult or obscure circumstances. They preferred to cross-examine a suspect repeatedly, often with considerable psychological finesse, in order to ascertain his motives as well as his words and deeds. They were quite capable of recommending the death penalty to secular authorities, who alone could kill even unrepentant heretics, and they handed out many harsh sentences short of the death penalty. Most of the time, however, these Inquisitors merely assigned penances of varying duration and intensity. Theirs was ultimately a culture of shame rather than a culture of violence. Given such values and procedures, it is not surprising that historians specialising in places as distant as Spanish America and northern Italy have independently pointed out the unique value of Inquisitorial records for understanding early modern cultural history, or that one of them has claimed that the Inquisitors 'were often using the same procedures as modern anthropologists in their fieldwork'.[12]

In order to grasp how Mediterranean Inquisitors actually

operated, how their patient questioning sometimes elucidated valuable ethnographic information about popular beliefs and 'superstitions', let us follow Carlo Ginzburg's account of an important episode, the first trial of a *benandante* in the Friuli, in 1580.[13] Battista Moduco, a middle-aged village crier, began his testimony by pointing out that he went regularly to confession, took communion, and knew no heretics. Asked whether he knew any witches or *benandanti*, he replied that he knew no *benandanti* except himself. The Inquisitor then asked what a *benandante* was; Moduco, after stalling a while, admitted boasting to several people that 'I go with the other *benandanti* to fight, four times a year, during the four seasons, at night, invisibly, with my spirit while my body stays; and we go in favour of Christ and the witches in favour of the Devil, fighting with each other, we using bundles of fennel and they use sticks of sorghum. . . . If we win, there is a good harvest, but shortages if we lose,' specifying that during different seasons these fights were over different crops.

Moduco claimed to have stopped being a *benandante* eight years earlier, since one entered this function at twenty and could be discharged at age forty. Everyone who was born with the caul (*camiscola*) around his neck was eligible for this service; Moduco said that at the age of twenty they were summoned with a drum, like draftees. The perplexed Inquisitor interrupted to ask why many gentlemen born with the *camiscola* were not *viandanti* (*sic*), but Moduco insisted that everyone who was born 'dressed' that way had to serve. Shifting his ground, the Inquisitor asked who assembled them. Moduco replied that it was a man like himself who summoned them with a drum. How many were there? Upwards of 5000, he said, some of them locals, others not. Who was their leader? 'I don't know,' came the reply, 'but I think he's sent by God, because we fight for the Christian faith.' Then the Inquisitor asked for names of other *benandanti*; but Moduco refused, just as he refused to name any witches, claiming that he had taken an oath of impartiality. The Inquisitor objected that if he were truly a soldier for Christ as he claimed, Moduco would reveal their names, especially since he was no longer active in this group. Eventually Battista named two witches, including a local woman who had reputedly dried up the milk from some cows. Here ends his first interrogation.

A second session three months later added relatively little.

Moduco, who had been jailed together with another *benandante*
whom he did not know, was now questioned primarily about
witches and their doings, but the question soon hit a dead-end.
Baffled, the Inquisitor tried a different tack, asking how this could
possibly be God's work, since men cannot by themselves become
invisible or separate their spirit from their body. Moduco's
response was first evasive ('They asked me so insistently, saying,
"Dear Battista, get up," and they were older than I') and then
repentant ('Yes sir, now I think this was a diabolical work, because
my companion told me so'). But then he began to ramble on about
how he had been reassured that he was doing God's work and that
those who died in this service would go straight to paradise; he
even described how, after their ritual battles, the *benandanti* and
witches on their way home sometimes stole into wineshops and
drank together (the witches pissed into the wine barrels afterwards). Finally, the exasperated Inquisitor interrupted to ask why
Moduco had said nothing about these activities to his confessor all
those years. 'I was afraid,' came the answer, because he had been
severely beaten just for talking to his friends about his nocturnal
exploits.

Moduco and his companion were liberated, but ordered to
remain at the Inquisition's disposal. After a long delay due to a
jurisdictional conflict, both men were finally sentenced in Novem-
ber 1581. Elements of possible heresy were emphasised, especially
Moduco's claim that *benandanti* went straight to heaven; his belief
that the captain of the *benandanti* had been chosen by God; and his
failure to say anything to his confessor. Both men were given
major excommunications and imprisoned for six months. They
were assigned various penances, particularly during the four
seasons, to repair the sins committed on those days. Their
sentences were then reduced – most Inquisitorial sentences have
two parts, with the second (and real) punishment being much
lighter than the first – to fifteen days' confinement to their
respective villages. After hearing the whole declaration amidst a
sizeable throng, both men solemnly abjured their errors.

A secular court would have interrogated and sentenced a man
like Moduco very differently. The major problem with his story
was the intimate association between *benandanti* and witches: how
could they possibly 'go out in spirit', leaving their bodies, in order
to meet, fight, and even fraternise with witches unless they were

somehow in association with them? Yet the Inquisitor never contemplated torturing Moduco in order to discover any possible dealings with the Devil. He interrogated him sometimes with superciliousness, but always with patience, trying to point out the contradictions in his account, and he ultimately devised a punishment that attempted to fit the crime. The whole business was treated as erroneous belief, rather than as apostasy.

Occasionally, when investigating witchcraft and related magical superstitions, Mediterranean Inquisitors went beyond routine interrogations and conducted true examinations. The most elaborate and impressive example occurred during the famous Basque witch panic of 1610 and beyond, when Inquisitor Salazar y Frias conducted a controlled experiment which is unique in the history of European witchcraft: Witches from one coven, selected from the most intelligent suspects, were led one by one to the place described as the site of their gatherings. They were not told where they were going, no other coven member was allowed to see them or learn anything about it beforehand. At the site of their meetings, each subject was questioned by a commissioner and notary about the exact location of the Sabbat, its distance from their homes, whether they travelled to it alone or in groups, how they left and re-entered their houses, whether they could hear clocks or bells during the Sabbat, and 'any other circumstances which might serve to clarify the problem and provide us with sure proofs of these things'. The experiment was then carried out, using three dozen confessed witches from nine different covens. When all interrogations had been completed, the answers were compared. In two instances all four answers agreed with each other. In the other seven they contradicted each other, and a few suspects admitted making false confessions. Salazar y Frias also collected samples of ointments used by witches to attend Sabbats and had them analysed by apothecaries. Twenty-two jars of powders, ointments and salves were tested. Several were fed to animals to see if they were poisonous; one was even eaten by a reputed witch in the presence of several witnesses. All proved harmless.[14]

This kind of experiment was never attempted by any secular court investigating witchcraft, not even the sceptical and highly sophisticated *parlementaires* of Paris who also became reluctant to condemn witches after about 1615. The amount of sobriety and seriousness in the Mediterranean Inquisitorial approach to superstitions is remarkable. They were proverbially slow, keeping prisoners confined or under investigation for years on end. But this slowness also demonstrated an unusual determination to avoid miscarriages of justice. In a type of law case where damages were spiritual rather than physical, the Inquisitions had to work slowly and grind exceeding fine. The remarkable popularity of the Inquisition, especially in Spain – a country famed for its litigousness, which reputedly governed its vast empire with few soldiers but many lawsuits – offers weighty testimony in favour of its general fairness. Its paternalism stood regorously opposed to all freedom of thought, but in the name of preserving the Catholic faith from erroneous and superstitious beliefs like Galileo's Copernicanism, which plainly contradicted Scripture. A Europe which considers classical liberalism *passé*, and which has learned how to use statistics had rediscovered the merits of these peculiar institutions of Mediterranean Catholicism. But a Europe which guiltily contemplates its history of Jewish-Christian relations also recognises their limitations.[15] To us, the Mediterranean Inquisitions remain Europe's most impressive models both of effective religious intolerance and of anti-magical 'enlightenment'.

Notes

1 The best general introduction to recent scholarship is the collection edited by J. Pérez Villanueva, *La Inquisición Española. Nueva Visión, nuevos horizontes* (Madrid, 1980); a useful sample has already appeared in French: Bartolomé Benassar (ed.), *L'Inquisition Espannole, XVe–XIXe siècle* (Paris, 1979).

2 J.-P. Dedieu, 'Les quatre temps de l'Inquisition', in Benassar, *L'Inquisition espagnole*, 29, 31.

3 The best introduction is by Charles Amiel, 'Les archives de l'Inquisition Portugaise', in *Arquivos de Centro Cultural Portuges de Paris* (Paris, 1979), 7–29. The computerisation of Portugal's excellently preserved central case files has already begun under the supervision of Robert Rowland and the patronage of the Gulbenkian Foundation.

4 See J.A. Tedeschi, 'Preliminary Observations on Writing a History of the Roman Inquisition', in F. Church and T. George (eds). *Continuity and discontinuity in Church History* (Leiden, 1979), 232–49; and Tedeschi's 'La dispersione degli archivi della Inquisizione romana', *Rivista distoria e letterature religiosa*, 9 (1973), 298–312.

5 Dedieu, 'Les quatre temps', 16–40; compare J. Veiga Torres, 'Uma longa guerra social: os ritmos da repressaõ inquisitorial em Portugal', *Revista de Historia Economica e Social*, ɪ (1978), 56–7.

6 See William Monter and John Tedeschi, 'Towards a Statistical Profile of the Italian Inquisitions, 1540–1790', (forthcoming).

7 Gustav Henningsen, *The Witches' Advocate: Basque Witchcraft and the Spanish Inquisition* (Las Vegas, 1980), 347; Monter-Tedeschi, 'Profile'.

8 Luisa Accati, 'Lo spirito della fornicazione: virtù dell' anima e virtù del corpo in Friuli fra '600 e '700', *Quaderni Storici*, 41 (1979), 669.

9 Gustav Henningsen, 'El banco de datos del Santo Oficio. Las relaciones de causas de la Inquisicion española (1550–1700)', *Boletín de la Real Academia de la Historia*, 174 (1977), 547–70; Ricardo Garcia Carcel, *Origenes de la Inquisición espanola: El tribunal de Valencia, 1478–1530* (Barcelona, 1976), 167–75; B. Benassar, 'L'Inquisition d'Aragon et al répression des pêchés "abominables"', in *L'Inquisition Espagnole*, 364.

10 The calculations of Amiel, 'Archives de l'Inquisition Portugaise', 23–4, fit well with those of Cecil Roth and H.C. Lea, *A History of the Marranos*, 3rd edn (London, 1958), 144–5. Amiel points out that about 10,000 trials never led to *Autos dafé*; if they are included, the Portuguese death rate falls to well under 3 per cent. See Monter-Tedeschi, 'Statistical Profile', for Italy.

11 See Paul Grendler, *The Roman Inquisition and the Venetian Press, 1540–1605* (Princeton, 1977); Henry Kamen, *The Spanish Inquisition* (London, 1965), 95–104, 257–66: Monter-Tedeschi, 'Statistical Profile'.

12 Quote from Gustav Henningsen, *Inquisition and Ethnography* (Copenhagen, 1973), English summary; see also Richard Greenleaf, 'The Mexican Inquisition and the Indians. Sources for the Ethnohistorian', *The Americas*, 34 (1978), 315–44: and especially Carlo Ginzburg, *The Cheese and the Worms* (Eng. trans.) (Baltimore, 1980).

13 Carlo Ginzburg, *The Benandanti* (Eng. trans.) (Baltimore, forthcoming) (Italian edn, 8–10, 14–18).

14 Henningsen, *Witches' Advocate*, 295–8.

15 Edward Glaser, 'Invitation to Intolerance: A Study of the Portuguese Sermons Preached at *Autos da fé*', *Hebrew Union College Annual*, 27 (1956), 327–85. Many such sermons were printed as pamphlets: see Rosemarie Horsch, *Sermões Impressos dos Autos de Fé* (Rio de Janeiro, 1969), for an inventory.

5 NORTHERN CATHOLICISM

Historians of the Catholic Reformation, whether traditionalists or revisionists, have always tended to see their subject as essentially monolithic, centralised, and relatively uniform. Its main outlines never vary: the significance of the Protestant Reformation and of indigenous reform traditions for the convocation of the Council of Trent; the epochal achievements of that Council; the establishment of the Society of Jesus, together with a cluster of other new Orders (amongst whom some, like the Capuchins and the Ursulines, were important in reshaping popular devotion); the struggles against Protestantism throughout Christendom, which by and large stopped the advance of heresy by 1580, and then reconquered much of central and eastern Europe during the following century; and last but far from least, the vigorous efforts to reform spiritual life in areas which remained, or again became, Catholic. Because the Tridentine decrees, *jus novissimum* in canon law, were universally applicable in Catholic lands, and because the Jesuits were ubiquitous both within and without Catholic lands, the Catholic Reformation has tended to be described in generalisations which leave little room for national or regional variations. And there were significant similarities even at the level of popular Catholicism which transcended national boundaries during the seventeenth and eighteenth centuries – things as small as pious householders reciting their Rosary on their front steps, in places as distant as Lisbon and Naples; or things as large as the simultaneous vogue of Black Madonnas at widely distant national pilgrimage shrines (Einsiedeln in Switzerland, Mariazell in Austria, Czestochowe in Poland). But there were also enormous differences between various parts of post-Tridentine Catholicism, discrepancies almost as great as those between Lutherans and Reformed Protestants. A Spanish officer rescued from the wreck of the

Armada by a colleen from Donegal reported that she was 'a Christian in like manner as Mahomet'. Even within a country enormous differences could exist. Perhaps the best-known example is the contrast between the 'two Italies', the austere piety of St. Carlo Borromeo's Milan, and the semi-pagan backwaters of the Kingdom of Naples which were explored by scandalised Jesuit missionaries in the mid-seventeenth century.[1]

Within Catholicism, the implementation of Tridentine reforms was never a simple, linear process proceeding more rapidly in some places and more slowly in others. It was even partially reversible. Consider the history of a key institution of lay piety from medieval Europe – the confraternity. In France, where the outlines of its history are best-known, confraternities suffered a sharp decline in numbers and activities during the late sixteenth century, even in predominantly Catholic regions like Champagne. During the seventeenth century, confraternities, like so much else in French religious life, revived, but also came under increasingly strict clerical supervision and control. Their non-religious elements, such as annual banquets, were abolished; while their traditional functions as burial associations were curtailed. The goal was to reduce confraternities from extended brotherhoods or social organisations to groups meeting solely for collective devotions. However, in remote corners of France, like the diocese of Tarbes, over two-thirds of all confraternities still had highly traditional statutes as late as 1700, while very few were purely devotional. And during the eighteenth century, at least in the well-explored region of Provence which had unusually large numbers of confraternities, they were progressively abandoned by social élites in favour of organisations with social, political, and quasi-religious functions: the Freemasons.[2]

The single most important difference within Catholic Europe after the counal of Trent was the presence or absence of an autonomous Inquisition which controlled both heretical and impious behaviour, punishing both adherents of different religions and ignorant Catholics who did not properly understand their own. North of the Alps and Pyrenees, no such institutions existed during the early modern period. Here, even heretics tended to be tried in secular courts, like the *Chambre ardente* ('court of fire') created by the *Parlement* of Paris in 1549, or the even more notorious Council of Troubles created by the Duke of Alva in the

Netherlands in 1567. Similarly, the most dangerous form of magical superstition, *maleficium*, belonged to secular rather than church courts throughout northern Europe; the last known hold out, the *Parlement* of Franche-Comté, still returned accused witches to ecclesiastical tribunals as late as 1596, but was judging such cases itself three years later.[3] Given such different institutional arrangements, both confessional coexistence and the repression of harmful magic assumed very different forms in Mediterranean and in northern Catholicism in the centuries after Trent.

Moreover, northern Catholicism was less internally uni-form than in the Mediterranean, partly because sizeable numbers of northern Catholics lived under Protestant governments. Not only was the political situation of an Irish Catholic totally different from that of a Bavarian Catholic, but the Irishman's religious traditions were also sharply different from the Bavarian's; a Dutch Catholic inhabited both a political situation and a cultural-religious environment quite different from either of them. It was not simply the absence of a nationwide Inquisition, but also the presence of different customs and institutions within its component parts which makes the concept of 'northern Catholicism' almost as fragmented as that of 'Reformed Protestantism'. Not even the uniformity of Tridentine legislation or the ubiquity of the Society of Jesus could flatten out the major differences within it. In this essay we shall try to define and compare its most important regional sub-divisions during the centuries between Luther and Voltaire.

The history of Austrian Catholicism was basically congruent with that of eastern Europe, much of which was governed from Vienna. Its most capable recent historian, R.J.W. Evans, confidently asserts that 'in everything from the choice of Christian names to the wording of epitaphs...the ethos of the Austrian Habsburg lands around 1550 was Protestant'. He offers such remarkable evidence as a monastic census for Lower Austria in 1563, which showed a total of 122 convents holding 463 monks, 200 concubines, 55 wives and 443 children. But the Habsburg emperors themselves remained Catholic, and during the seven-teenth century a totally reinvigorated Catholicism suffused their Austrian provinces, snuffing out Protestantism more slowly and less dramatically than in Bohemia, but more rapidly and far more successfully than in Hungary. In a remote corner of Lower Austria, a reconversion campaign netted 22,000 new Catholics as late as the 1650s, and Lutherans were not expelled from the lands of the Archbishop of Salzburg until the 1730s. But the overall success of the Counter-Reformation and baroque piety in Austria was so complete that it requires a considerable effort of the historical imagination to recapture here (as in Poland) the extent of Protestantism among its nobility and burghers during the Renaissance.

By 1700 the triumph of Catholic orthodoxy seemed complete. The hereditary Austrian lands, worked over by Jesuit and Capuchin preachers, supplied with seminaries, catechisms and other implements of Tridentine persuasion, blossomed forth with a profusion of rebuilt baroque monasteries and many other signs of older and newer devotions. Leading the way among the older forms was the Virgin Mary, to whom the Emperor Ferdinand III had consecrated his hereditary lands through the Immaculate Conception. By 1700 Austria boasted major pilgrimage shrines not only to the Black Madonna of Mariazell (which drew over 125,000 pilgrims annually during the eighteenth century), but also to Maria Taferl near the great monastery at Melk, or Mariastein in the Tyrol. The most popular of the newer devotions was St John Nepomuk, an obscure fourteenth-century Czech martyr who was finally beatified under Habsburg pressure in 1723. Of fifty-four statues erected in the diocese of Vienna during the late seventeenth and early eighteenth century, thirty-one were of him, mostly made between 1720 and 1740 (in the same period there were only six new statues of the Virgin and two of Christ). Regarded as a martyr of the confessional and patronised by the Jesuits throughout the Austrian Empire, Nepomuk was believed to possess thaumaturgical powers and to offer protection against floods or fires. The list of popular Austrian baroque saints also included a totally spurious one (St Domitian) who became the patron of the province of Carinthia: he helped to avoid disease and to catch fish.

Counter-Reformation Austria also occupied an unusual place in the general history of European witch-hunting. Well over a third of its 1700 surviving trials took place between 1670 and 1690; the peak of Austrian witch-hunting occurred between 1650 and 1715 – later than almost everywhere in western Europe, but slightly earlier than in Poland or Hungary. Considering that the trials described in the *Malleus Maleficarum* happened in Austria, it seems strange that so few were held there between 1590 and 1630, when they were common throughout Europe. Austrian trials after 1660 amounted to a social war against beggars of all types from children to old crones, but especially against demobilised soldiers. The largest cluster of trials, held at Salzburg from 1675 to 1681, reads like a meeting between an outlaw motorcycle gang and Dr Faustus: a blood-brotherhood of highwaymen and swindlers, known as the *Zauberjäckl* or magic-jacket gang, replete with homosexuality, desecrations of the Host, werewolves, and the magical transformations of mice. In all, about 180 people were accused, half of them under the age of twenty. By 1678 the Archbishop of Salzburg had to forbid the execution of children under twelve for such crimes. The other famous Austrian trials, from Feldbach (Styria), featured a priest who performed Black Masses, baptised his parishioners' children in the Devil's name, and kept a concubine who was able to grow fresh flowers in mid-winter. Witch-trials provide the obverse of a triumphant Austrian baroque.[5]

During the *Zauberjäckl* trials, the treatises of a Styrian physician, Adam von Lebenwaldt, were published in Salzburg, offering the most complete Austrian attack on popular superstitions. Like Austria's greatest preacher, Abraham a Sancta Clara, von Lebenwaldt was wholly sympathetic to the witch-hunters. He poured scorn on Kabbalists, and had little use for astrology, but he was a Paracelsian who clearly did not consider alchemy any more superstitious than witchcraft. In general, Austrian baroque culture was sympathetic towards most forms of learned magic, at the same time that it was scornful of popular magic and very strict towards witchcraft. In a region which had been reclaimed from Protestantism there was little room to attack the miraculous or the supernatural. Austrian scepticism was confined to very narrow circles in Vienna, often foreigners around Prince Eugene, until a few Jansenist prelates emerged in the mid-eighteenth century to attack the excessive use of ritual and ceremonies. Soon afterwards came the revolutionary Emperor Joseph ii who promulgated literally thousands of religious changes throughout the Habsburg lands – but with him we enter a different age.

In the texture of its baroque piety, Bavaria seems little different from Austria. Famous preachers, impressive new buildings, devotional shrines to old and new cults, marked its religious climate throughout the Tridentine era. One interesting regional nuance was the Bavarian fondness for horse-pilgrimages, or *Umritte*, which developed during the seventeenth century, and reached its ultimate pinnacle in 1756, when more than 7000 horsemen participated in a Holy Blood *Umritt* at a Bavarian monastery. But there were other and more important ways in which Bavaria differed from Austria. The Counter-Reformation arrived remarkably early in Bavaria, where it was rigorously controlled from the outset by secular authorities. In 1558, five years before the close of Trent, Duke Albrecht v began to carry out religious visitations in his territories. He soon imposed censorship on the model of the Roman Index, and in 1570 he created a College of Ecclesiastical Councillors as the supreme authority for all Bavarian ecclesiastical matters. Its archives hold hundreds of library catalogues submitted by priests whose orthodoxy was questioned, thousands of annual 'inquisitions' conducted in every Bavarian parish to identify crypto-Protestants, freethinkers, or other deviants, and individual dossiers on these nonconformists. All in all, this institution and its records offer the closest approximation to the files of a Mediterranean Inquisition to be found north of the Alps. By the seventeenth century, Maximilian I of Bavaria went further, and ordered this College to examine all schoolchildren annually in order to judge what they actually understood of their catechisms – a practice not done even in Spain. Maximilian searched through book dealers' lodgings, paid spies, fined people who failed to report suspicious acts, and finally, in 1629, named a central commission headed by his Jesuit confessor to conduct an Inquisition in Bavaria, thus bringing a certain Teutonic thoroughness to the repressive system of post-Tridentine Catholicism.[6]

Such measures worked. By the late sixteenth century Bavaria had no serious Protestant problem. Although her struggle against heretics was as vigilant as in Italy or Spain, Bavaria and its crypto-Inquisition did not share the lenient attitudes of the south, which regarded even maleficient witchcraft as superstition. Here, like everywhere else in the north, witches were tried before secular tribunals in sizeable numbers. Despite old legends dating from the *Kulturkampf*, Bavaria was not unusually virulent in its witch-hunting. In the mammoth collection of German witch trials assembled by Heinrich Himmler, the Duchy of Bavaria accounted for about 500 cases out of 30,000 – which, considering its size and population, is below average for the Empire.[7] The relative success of Bavaria's mission as the bastion of German Catholicism, untainted by Austria's sixteenth-century waverings, may have contributed to the moderation of its witch-hunts.

Catholicism in the Rhine basin, the long narrow strip between France and the Empire which had long ago formed Lotharingia, also had some original features. Here no important centralised states could give direction and control to religious policies towards either heresy or supersition: the southern Netherlands and Franche-Comté were largely autonomous within the Habsburg orbit, while Lorraine and the three Rhenish archepiscopal Electorates were fully independent. These middle-sized territories had no serious domestic problems with Protestantism after 1590, although all of them lived in close proximity to Protestant governments, particularly to three Reformed states – Switzerland to the south, the United Netherlands to the north, and the Palatinate in between. The region's Catholicism was relatively archiac because of its institutional backwardness, yet combative with a frontier mentality because of the Protestant presence nearby.

Lotharingian Catholicism was a major centre of European witchcraft. From the south-western German corner of Baden-Wurttemberg, so well described by Erik Midelfort, through the 'priests' alley', up to Luxemburg ran a chain of lands obsessed by the phenomenon of witchcraft. Several demonologists, led by a suffragan Bishop of Trier and a chief prosecutor of the Duchy of Lorraine, lived and worked in this region. This preoccupation permeated all levels of local society. In Luxemburg, a priest was denounced by his congregation in 1616 as a 'great magician' because he had preached that accused witches should be set free, following the scriptural principle that it was worse to kill the innocent than to spare the guilty; he had even threatened witch-hunters with eternal damnation. (The priest managed to clear himself by producing a witness who testified that none of his sermons was heretical.) There were differences between French- and German-speaking Lotharingia. In bilingual Luxemburg, the five Germanic districts tried 316 witches and executed 260, while the six French districts tried 122 and executed only 65; in bilingual Lorraine, the 465 executions from its German-speaking quarter seem disproportionately large. Binsfeld's Bishopric of Trier seems to have been afflicted by worse witch-hunts than Boguet's Franche-Comté, using more torture and recording more 'accomplices' named by confessing witches. But such differences in degree should not obscure the general similarity in kind: witch-hunting was unusually severe in Catholic Lotharingia.[8]

Religious practices in this region seem somewhat archiac. For instance, the religious history of Lorraine is dotted with personages like a pious ex-soldier turned hermit, who translated the great Spanish mystics into French at his retreat near Nancy for thirty years, or a devout widow who founded the Order of Refuge and was almost beatified: she not only levitated, distributed curative medallions and healed by touch, but also suffered from eight years of demonic possession during which she had engineered the death of her physician for bewitching her. Collective devotions in this duchy reached their apogee on 6 May 1642, when its capital city organised a special pilgrimage after a severe winter. More than 2000 citizens divided into nine social cohorts to symbolise the nine angelic choruses, marched for four days to the shrine of Our Lady of Benoîte-Vaux. At the shrine, during the Elevation, the President of Lorraine's tax court prostrated himself before the altar, expiatory candle in hand, making public amends for the sins of all; after mass, he announced that the capital city had been consecrated to the Virgin, and the whole duchy placed under her protection. Lorraine's *via moderna* was Jansenism, which arrived quite late, remained a purely theological movement led by bishops, and survived in significant ways into the twentieth century.[9]

Our tour of northern Catholicism has thus far been confined to places where this Church was officially established. Conditions of Catholic life were radically different in areas controlled by Protestants, where Catholics were usually perceived as disloyal subjects, and their religious organisation was clandestine. Although unofficial, this part of northern Catholicism was far from insignificant. One of its finest seventeenth-century theologians, Jansenius, was born in Utrecht: while Ireland offers a wonderful laboratory in which to see Tridentine reforms at work among a rural Catholic population whose state apparatus was entirely Protestant.[10]

Dutch Catholicism was marked by the same sober inwardness that had once produced the *devotio moderna* and the *philosophia Christi*. Its post-Tridentine hierarchy was rigorously opposed to all forms of Jesuit laxity, and the Mission which governed it always included many more secular clergy than missionary regulars. Many important Dutch artists were Catholics, but there was no Dutch Catholic art. In this country we can learn little about confraternities or pilgrimages, but much about Bible-reading in the vernacular among Catholics: five Dutch New Testaments and three complete Dutch Bibles were produced especially for Catholics between 1646 and 1657. A defensive Puritanism seems to be the dominant tone, making the country a logical refuge for French Jansenists who virtually took over the Dutch Mission during the eighteenth century.

Ireland was completely different: an underdeveloped land whose pre-Tridentine Church lacked a satisfactory parish structure or regular religious observance. Here a combination of missionary clergy and reforming bishops began to introduce modern Catholicism to the island between the 1590s and the 1640s. They were handicapped less by the English Protestant establishment than by the customs of the Irish, who could not be organised into watertight parishes in which regular confession and Easter attendance could be expected. The Irish persisted in their habits of clan feuds and riotous wakes, which raised problems outside the scope of Tridentine legislation. They also continued to practice polygamy, divorce, and incestuous marriage. Despite the obstacles involved in working clandestinely, Catholic reformers had made some progress by the mid-seventeenth century – at least, it now became realistic to expect Irish priests to refuse confession to anyone ignorant of the four basic prayers or the ten commandments.

The kingdom of France was perhaps the most important region in northern Catholicism. Equipped with the oldest and most respected theological faculty in Christendom, with the strongest national-church movement within Catholicism, and with a thaumaturgical king who was 'touching' thousands of his subjects at a time as late as the 1690s, France obviously offers some interesting features. It was also the largest country to experience almost ninety years of official coexistence between the Catholic and Reformed Churches, and the last major country to end such coexistence.

Considering its size, France experienced relatively few prosecutions for harmful witchcraft. Over half the kingdom lived under the appellate jurisdiction of the *Parlement* of Paris, which was remarkably careful and lenient when judging accusations of this crime. Between 1564 and 1640, it upheld only 115 of 474 death sentences for it, and released over 400 accused witches. Despite the shrill pleas of a famous political theorist, Jean Bodin, in his *Démonomanie des sorciers* (1580), the *Parlement* of Paris remained scarcely more horrified by this crime than were the great Mediterranean Inquisitions; it was far more severe towards accused arsonists, homosexuals, or infanticides, than towards sorcerers. Of course, as French historians have observed, witchcraft was more important on the kingdom's periphery than at its centre, so as yet untabulated prosecutions from France's eight regional *parlements* would probably show greater legal severity towards accused witches than at Paris. But Paris set the tone; and even in the worst French provincial situations, prosecutions were milder than in French-speaking parts of the Holy Roman Empire. The Basque panic of 1608–10, led by the Bordeaux judge and demonologist Pierre de Lancre, saw eighty people executed in three years – a sizeable number, but well below the thousands from Nicholas Remy's Lorraine.[11]

If the judicial history of witchcraft in sixteenth and seventeenth century France seems relatively enlightened, the political history of French witchcraft has its uniquely sinister side. France was the only European nation with a series of show trials of demonically-possessed women between 1562 and 1634, all manipulated on behalf of some political purpose. The list began with a demoniac whose exorcists used a consecrated Host to expel the demons, thus scoring a point against the Huguenot doctrine of the Eucharist at the outbreak of France's religious wars. At the end of these wars came another case in 1599, where exorcists reinforced the campaign against religious toleration just decreed by the Edict of Nantes. Afterwards, political dissidents replaced Protestants as exorcists' scapegoats, thus starting a new series which culminated with France's most famous show trial, involving the execution of a Jesuit for bewitching an entire Ursuline convent. During these exorcisms the devils repeatedly blasphemed God and the angels, but never said a word against the King or Cardinal Richelieu. Richelieu himself, describing the episode in his memoirs, equivocated:

Because there is so much deception in this matter and because simplicity, which ordinarily accompanies piety, often makes people believe things of this kind which aren't true, the Cardinal didn't dare fix a solid judgement on the report made to him. . . . But at last this business became so public, and so many nuns became possessed, that the Cardinal, who could not ignore the complaints made to him from all sides, advised the king to interpose his authority

Techniques of manipulation had not improved since 1562, and the puppeteer's hands were still visible on the strings. Cynics and sceptics, frequently vocal throughout French history, made objections during these trials. Protestants detected fraud; physicians diagnosed hysteria; and judges were sometimes unimpressed. On the other hand, such spectacles were highly edifying. Huguenots converted after watching successful exorcisms, or a king's reprobate brother would promise to reform. Despite (or because of) these cross-currents, such show trials were more important in France than anywhere else.[12]

Another religious development concentrated in France was the rise of Jansenism during the 'century of saints' and implementation of Tridentine reforms. French historians agree that the significance of Jansenism was totally disproportionate to the numbers of true Jansenists – fifty to sixty nuns at Port-Royal, flanked by a dozen or so *solitaires*. To us, the most curious and important aspect of French Jansenism was the official response to it. The 'men of order', Richelieu and Louis xiv, vehemently opposed a movement of austerity which strenuously condemned frivolity and religious disorder. Although neither Richelieu nor much less Louis xiv ever understood its theology, the French state proved unremittingly hostile towards Jansenism from Richelieu's arrest of St-Cyran in 1638 to Louis' forced dispersion of Port-Royal's nuns, desecration of its buildings, violations of its tombs, and demolition of the convent itself between 1709 and 1712. To them Jansenism seemed subversive. A major Catholic state which tolerated the Reformed Church and subsidised its Protestant allies distrusted this faction's moral absolutism which despised reason of state. But among the French clergy the Jansenist movement also stimulated the most thorough and successful efforts to uproot local superstitions while implementing Tridentine reforms.

Apart from its policies towards *possédées*, or Jansenists, France is important to students of early modern Catholicism because it is the home of historical religious sociology. Its ecclesiastical historians have been concerned with measurements as well as with devotional literature, and their numerous recent monographs (usually at the diocesan level) have generally contained statistical components which attempt to describe the history of religious practice. Considering the peculiarities of France within Catholic Europe, it seems hazardous to extrapolate French results to other Catholic lands; but since this is by far the best explored region for the historian of popular religious practices, France requires special attention.

Nearly all these monographs agree that the Tridentine reforms were successfully implemented during the seventeenth century, with important consequences for both religious beliefs and social customs. Their cumulative effect produced a phenomenon described by Peter Burke as the 'triumph of Lent', and by Jean Delumeau as the delayed Christianisation of Europe. The former aspect is less paradoxical and easier to grasp. It could be as simple and graphic as the parish priest of a village near Paris routing a group of travelling actors in the 1640s:

I remember, one holiday, being warned that some actors were performing a farce on a stage they had built, that I went there with some officers of the law, climbed up on the stage, ripped the mask off the principal actor, seized and broke the violin from the person playing it, and chased them off the stage which the officers then broke up; since that time, no strolling players have dared come to Nanterre.

Multiply such incidents by a hundred, add the elimination of profane activities within churches or cemeteries and the reductions in the numbers and celebrations of holidays. But the triumph of Lent remained incomplete, and its achievements could always be threatened. As late as 1740, a priest noted for his austere sermons was mocked on Ash Wednesday by a masked group parading a straw priest on a donkey, asking if it would preach; when its head nodded, the dummy was whipped and finally burned on the village square.[13]

Delumeau's thesis that an educated Christianity began only in early modern Europe, 'between Luther and Voltaire', seems more provocative. His argument rests on some close parallels between Protestant and Catholic styles of religious instruction, and on a fundamental division between medieval Christianity – heavily encrusted with relics of paganism and an animist mentality, administered by an overly numerous but undertrained clergy – and post-Reformation religion, based on grassroots religious instruction among the laity on a scale never previously attempted. 'After a millenium of assimilating animism came a total rejection of it, and the religion of a few was to be imposed on millions.' The awareness of 'idolatry' and 'superstition' was no monopoly of Protestants. The Council of Trent had protested against adoration of images and against magical interpretations of numbers in the service, especially numbers of masses and candles. Catholic missionaries and reforming bishops, claims Delumeau, spoke a language similar to that of many Protestant officials.[14]

If we attempt to assess the results of this educational campaign by comparing popular Catholicism of the mid-eighteenth century not with Protestantism but with fifteenth-century Catholicism, we obtain the following picture:

1. Several important Catholic practices remained basically unchanged after Trent. The seven sacraments were undisturbed by Protestant criticism, and the demand for a prompt, precise, and cheap administration of them remained a basic desire of the Catholic laity. Similarly, many important trends of late medieval devotion were either unchanged or reinforced in Catholic Europe after Trent. For instance, the wave of Marian devotion, visible in the newer shrines of fifteenth-century Europe, persisted and sometimes even accelerated. In 1652 Bohemia contained only two shrines to the Virgin, but by the eighteenth century there were forty-four. In the French diocese where Our Lady of Lourdes now draws multitudes of pilgrims, the seven important shrines restored after the Wars of Religion were all Marian. Pilgrimages to such shrines, often in search of miraculous cures, seem to have revived and even increased after a sixteenth-century decline in several places. The doctrine of

purgatory, still gaining momentum in the fifteenth century, reached its apogee in southern France around 1700; *post-mortem* masses intended to reduce time in purgatory (which however is almost never named in testaments) were even more widespread around 1700 than they had been two centuries earlier, both at Paris and in southern France. Brussels commemorated the semi-centennials of its 1370 bleeding Host miracle (and ensuing death of all local Jews) in 1670, 1720 and 1770 'with a fanfare merited by a better cause', while the sale of bogus indulgences remained a significant problem for the Holy Office of Naples during the seventeenth and even the eighteenth centuries.[15]

2. Other aspects of post-Tridentine Catholicism show improvements rather than continuities. Under this heading comes increased attendance at liturgical events, led as before by Easter. In the late middle ages many people had missed Easter communion either through laziness or excommunication, but remarkably few did so after Trent. In the archdeaconry of Paris, only 112 of 50,000 adults in 137 parishes missed Easter in 1672. Other major holy days also seem to have been better attended. In a rural Flemish deanery, half of all adults took communion at other holidays besides Easter during the seventeenth century. Meanwhile the number of official holidays was reduced by about one-third. 'Less is more' appears in another important context: all accounts agree that the number of clergy, both regular and secular, declined after Trent, but their educational preparation and their median incomes rose. Finally, tighter control of sex and marriage also had important effects at the parish level after Trent. Clerical concubinage almost disappeared. So did illegitimacy among the laity, although the average age at first marriage rose to unprecedented heights during seventeenth and eighteenth centuries: around 1700 the fully-developed 'European marriage pattern' was accompanied by record lows of bastardy throughout most of Catholic (and Protestant) Europe.[16]

3. Finally, some aspects of Tridentine Catholicism demonstrate clear novelties in comparison with the late middle ages. Two seem especially important: missions and catechisms. The latter were adapted from Protestant practice after a brief delay (St Peter Canisius's effort followed thirty years after Luther's), but attained their fullest development only later: between 1670 and 1685 more than twenty diocesan catechisms were published in

France. One of the best-known combined a children's catechism in twenty-seven pages, a preparatory catechism for first communion in ninety-three pages, and a 382-page 'great catechism' for educated laity and priests. Teaching these catechisms, usually on Sunday evenings, became a new and onerous duty for parish priests, as the massive visitation records of the seventeenth and eighteenth centuries attest. Other religious instruction was also given in primary schools, which remained under clerical supervision in both Catholic and Protestant Europe. These were often run by the newer religious orders, like the Ursuline nuns or the Brothers of St Jean Baptiste de la Salle.[17]

Catechisms and schooling were follow-ups to the fieldwork of post-Tridentine missionaries. Some of their methods were borrowed from earlier revivalists – the 'holy bonfires' of Savonarola's age, for instance, were used in Normandy by St John Eudes in the 1670s – but early modern missionaries, unlike medieval friars, worked in rural rather than in urban districts, and thus had to develop several new techniques. By the mid-seveteenth century Catholic missionary activity had almost become a science, practised by experienced teams who remained in villages for weeks at a time, until all adults had gone to confession and even the thickest witted had at least learned the Ave, the Paternoster and the Credo well enough to recite them twice a day. Tridentine missionaries used many forms of propaganda, from pasteboard allegorical pictures to pious parodies of love-songs or drinking-songs, but always with sermons at their centre in order to provoke a salutary fear of God, and desire for penance in these rustics' hearts.

How justified is the optimism of Delumeau, who claims that 'at the parish level, the Catholic enlightenment was at once the rejection of superstition, an attempt to purify worship and give the faithful a more active part in it, and a determination to instruct the faithful'? Most Catholic authorities, from parish priests upwards, thought this indoctrination was working with most of the people most of the time. Many possible forms of measurement – Easter attendance, illegitimacy rates, clerical incomes, numbers of pilgrims attending major shrines – can be cited to buttress this assessment. Listen to a parish priest from the diocese of Tournai, describing his flock around 1690:[18]

As for the parish, there is scarcely any advance in their amendment, although by God's grace we never fail to preach during high Mass on Sundays or holidays, or to catechise after Vespers whenever the *curé's* health permits. Concerning religion and the articles of faith, there is no one capable of sustaining the contrary of what is preached. But as this village was formerly neglected during the wars, there are still some who nourish old errors in their hearts, which they maintain only because they have heard it from their fathers, and which they maintain *mordicus*, as for example that one can be saved in any kind of religion. The second fault of these parishioners is a certain negligence or lukewarmness about matters of salvation. For instance, they are extremely negligent about taking the sacraments of attending holy services in their parish. They have no scruples about missing Mass, they are negligent to the point of scorn about attending Vespers, especially in good weather; because in winter, when they have nothing better to do, they come, but always late, and whenever it's good weather you cannot find enough people to ring the bells.

Clerical optimism was tempered by 'old errors which they still nourish in their hearts' about Protestants going to Heaven, something which never turns up in statistics about seventeenth-century Catholic religious practices. When dealing with Tridentine Catholicism, as with early modern Protestantism, we can usually see much more clearly into the minds of the reformers than into those of their audience.

There are two important caveats to set against the optimistic view of Tridentine Catholicism. First, we must not exaggerate the extent of rationalism within Delumeau's 'Catholic Enlightenment'. This was still a world of the miraculous, where peasants from western France were 'Gospelled' in front of a saint's statue by priests who placed both ends of their stole over the pilgrim's head while reading a page of the Gospel or the prayer to that particular saint; where German peasants (including a few Protestants) flocked to get *Xavierus wasser* to protect their cattle against epidemics; where Italians suffering from leprosy plunged into the ocean on Holy Saturday to the sound of church bells; or where eastern French villagers sent no fewer than 120 requests to the Archbishop of Besançon between 1729 and 1762 requesting formulae for exorcisms to use against insects and rodents. Opposing Delumeau's view, another French Catholic historian argued that Tridentine reforms had indeed restored and improved religious practice, and here and there had advanced a more enlightened religion. But we must not be deceived by these positive results. For many people in Anjou, Christianity remained at the outbreak of the French Revolution what it had been in the seventeenth and earlier centuries: one of the elements in a popular religion where faith and superstition were inextricably mixed.

Throughout the era after Trent the Catholic Church had to walk an extremely fine line between genuine and bogus miracles, between angelic and demonic visions. Proudly denying the Protestant assertion that the age of miracles had passed, Catholics remained vulnerable to criticisms that their religion could never rid itself of supersitious practices.[19]

Secondly, there were signs that the impressive façade of post-Tridentine Catholicism had begun to crack and peel badly after 1750. Studies of testaments and confraternities in eighteenth-century Provence showed that commemorative masses declined sharply after 1760, while the leadership of penitential confraternities was seduced away into Freemasonry about the same time. Confraternities were also having problems in other parts of Catholic Europe. In Seville, which boasted over a thousand *cofradias*, many of them refused to participate in religious processions by 1780; at Lisbon, members of guild confraternities insisted they be paid while performing religious duties during working hours. These were grassroots problems, independent of the attacks on the whole idea of confraternities by Jansenist prelates and enlightened despots, which led to their abolition in Tuscany, Lombardy and Austria during the 1780s.[20] The edifice of Tridentine Catholicism was ultimately wrecked, not by revolutionary France but by the policies of 'enlightened' Catholic rulers who dismantled Inquisitions, abolished monasteries, and of course destroyed the Society of Jesus in 1772. But they could not have begun their wrecking if the movement itself had not already been spiritually exhausted.

Notes

1   See W. J. Callahan and D. Higgs (eds), *Church and Society in Catholic Europe of the Eithteenth Century* (Cambridge, 1979), 63, 73; John Bossy, 'The Counter-Reformation and the People of Catholic Ireland, 1596–1641', in *Historical Studies VIII: Papers of the Irish*

Conference of Historians (Dublin, 1971), 157. There is no comparative study of the three famous Black Madonnas. On the 'two Italies', compare Mgr Roncalli (the future Pope John xxiii) (ed.), *Gli atti della visita di S. Carlo Borromeo a Bergamo 1576*, 6 vols (Milan, 1936–49), with Gabriele de Rosa, *Vescovi, popolo e magia nel Sud: richerche di storia socio-religiosa dal XVII al XIX secolo* (Bari, 1971).

2 A.N. Galpern, *The Religions of the People in Sixteenth-Century Champagne* (Cambridge, Mass., 1976), 188–91, 203–13; Robert Harding 'The Mobilization of Confraternities against the Reformation in France', *Sixteenth Century Journal*, 11 (1980), 85–107; Y.-M. Bercé, *Fête et révolte* (Paris, 1976), 145–7; J.-F. Soulet, *Traditions et réformes religieuses dans les Pyrenées centrales au XVIIe siècle* (Pau, 1974), 263–8; Maurice Agulhon, *Pénitents et Franc-Maçons dans l'ancienne Provence* (Paris, 1968); Michel Vovelle, *Piété baroque et déchristianisation en Provence au XVIIIe siècle* (Paris, 1978), abridged edn), 154–64, 204–14.

3 William Monter, *Witchcraft in France and Switzerland* (Ithaca, 1976), 73 and n. 11.

4 R.J.W. Evans, *The Making of the Habsburg Monarchy, 1550–1700* (Oxford, 1979), 3 (quote), 119, 157–94; J. Bérenger, in Callahan-Higgs (n. 1), 101–5; H. Bachmann, *Das Mirakelbüch der Wallfahrtskirche Mariastein im Tyrol als Quelle zur Kulturgeschichte 1678–1742* (Munich-Innsbruck, 1973).

5 Fritz Byloff, *Hexenglaube und Hexenverfolgung in der österreichischen Alpenländern* (Berlin-Leipzig, 1934).

6 Max Spindler (ed.), *Handbuch der Bayerischen Geschichte*, 4 vols (Munich, 1967–75), ii, 626–56, 920–69. Gerald Strauss, *Luther's House of Learning* (Baltimore, 1978), 288–91, 381 n. 178, provides a good brief introduction to the College; see Lionel Rothkrug, *Religious Practices and Collective Perceptions: Hidden Homologies in the Renaissance and Reformation* (Waterloo, Ont., 1980), 66, on *Umritte*.

7 Gerhard Schormann, *Hexenprozesse in Deutschland* (Göttingen, 1981), 66.

8 Alois Hahn, *Die Rezeption des tridentinischen Pfarrideals im westtrierischen Pfarrklerus des 16. und 17. Jahrhunderts* (Luxemburg, 1974), 342; Marie-Sylvie Dupont-Bouchat, 'La Répression de la sorcellerie dans le Duché de Luxembourg aux XVIe et XVIIe siècles', in *Prophètes et sorciers dans les Pays-Bas, XVIe–XVIIIe siècle* (Paris, 1978), 127 – minus the French-speaking territories of St Hubert, Neufchâteau, and Bouillon, which did not belong to Luxemburg; Henri Hiegel, *Le Bailliage d'Allemagne de 1600 à 1632* (Saarguemines, 1961), 188–222; and the major synthesis of Etienne Delcambre, *Le Concept de la sorcellerie dans le Duché de Lorraine aux XVIe et XVIIe siècles*, 3 vols (Nancy, 1949–51).

9 René Taveneaux, *Le Jansenisme en Lorraine, 1640–1789* (Paris, 1960); and the brilliant summary by Pierre Chaunu, 'Jansenisme et frontière de catholicité (xviie et xviiie siècles)', *Revue historique* (January–March 1962), 115–38; René Taveneaux, *Le Catholicisme dans la France classique, 1610–1715*, 2 vols (Paris, 1980), i, 87; ii, 380–1; Étienne Delcambre, *Un Cas énigmatique de possession diabolique en Lorraine au xviie siècle: Elisabeth de Ranfaing* (Nancy, 1956).

10 Cf. Bossy, 'Counter-Reformation and People of Ireland' (n. 1); and L.-J. Rogier and P. Brachin, *Histoire du catholicisme hollandais depuis le xvie siècle* (Paris, 1974), 21–75.

11 Alfred Soman, 'The *Parlement* of Paris and the Great Witch-Hunt (1565–1640)', *Sixteenth-Century Journal*, 9 (1978), 31–45, which corrects the thesis of Robert Mandrou, *Magistrats et sorciers en France au xviie siècle* (Paris, 1968); also Gustav Henningsen, *Basque Witchcraft and the Spanish Inquisition* (Las Vegas, 1980), 25.

12 D.P. Walker, *Unclean Spirits: Possession and Exorcism in France and England in the late Sixteenth and early Seventeenth Centuries* (Philadelphia, 1981); Aldous Huxley, *The Devils of Loudun* (London, 1952), 156; Michel de Certeau, *La Possession de Loudun* (Paris, 1971), 109–11.

13 Peter Burke, *Popular Culture in Early Modern Europe* (London, 1978), ch. 8; Taveneaux, *Catholicime en France classique*, ii, 330–1; René Taveneaux, *La Vie quotidienne des Jansenistes* (Paris, 1974), 120.

14 Jean Delumeau, *Catholicism between Luther and Voltaire*, (London, 1977), 129–202; quote from Delumeau's 1975 inaugural lecture at the *Collège de France*, 19.

15 Callahan-Higgs (n. 1), 102; J.-F. Soulet, *Traditions et réformes* (n. 2), 250–65; G. and M. Vovelle, *Vision de la mort et de l'au-delà en Provence, d'après les autels des âmes du purgatoire xve–xixe siècles* (Paris, 1970), 22–37; M. Vovelle, *Piété baroque* (n. 2), ch. 3; Pierre Chaunu, *La Mort à Paris, 16e, 17e, 18e siècle* (Paris, 1977), 386–7, 409–17; Salo Baron, *A Social and Religious History of the Jews*, 17 vols (New York, 1852–76), x, 19; William Monter and John Tedeschi, 'Towards a Statistical Profile of the Italian Inquisition' forthcoming.

16 Taveneaux, *Catholicisme en France classique*, ii, 342–3; M. Cloet, 'Religious Life in a Rural Deanery in Flanders during the Seventeenth Century: Tielt from 1609 to 1700', *Acta Historica Neerlandiae*, 5 (1971), 135–58; Jean-Louis Flandrin, *Families in Former Times* (Cambridge, 1979), ch. 4; Michael W. Flinn, *The European Demographic System, 1500–1820*, in this series.

17 Delumeau, *Catholicism from Luther to Voltaire*, 189–202.

18 Henri Platelle (ed.), *Journal d'un curé de campagne au xviie siècle* (Paris, 1965), 76–7; Delumeau, *Luther to Voltaire*, 202.

19 François Lebrun, *Les Hommes et la mort en Anjou aux XVIIe et XVIIIe siècles*, (Paris, 1975 abridged edn), 287, 299; Callahan-Higgs, 75; Victor-L. Tapié, *The Age of Grandeur: Baroque Art and Architecture* (London, 1960), 154–5; Delumeau, *Luther to Voltaire*, 170.

20 Callahan-Higgs, 46–7, 58–60, 71, 94, 151–2; Vovelle, *Piété baroque* (n. 2), ch. 3; Agulhon (n. 2).

Bibliographical Note

A fundamental article, comparable in scope to Strauss's essay on 'Success and Failure in the German Reformation', is John Bossy's, 'The Counter-Reformation and the People of Catholic Europe', *Past and Present*, 47 (1970), 51–70.

6 COEXISTENCE AND SUPERSTITION IN THE AMERICAS

The Spanish conquest of America was religious as well as political. Within a remarkably short time, and with very small numbers of monastic *conquistadores*, the pre-Tridentine Castilian Church laid extremely durable foundations for the Catholicisation of Central and South America. The rapid acculturation of the former worshippers of Quetzalcoatl and Huitzlipochtli was followed by a far slower and less complete Christianisation in the other parts of Iberian America: Peru and Brazil proved harder nuts to crack, while the missionary frontier edged its way north-west from the old Aztec heartlands throughout the eighteenth century. Everywhere in the Catholic regions of colonial America, from Canada to Chile, there was a strong and persistent missionary drive which was almost completely absent from the Protestant colonies which dotted several parts of the Americas after the early 1600s. Yet all European colonists, regardless of nationality, religion, or missionary impulses, shared an innate sense of the moral superiority of Christianity, and an often ill-concealed disgust at the pagan superstitions of the Amerindians. Throughout the colonial Americas, from Conquest to Independence, the conflict between European and indigenous religions was real, but the balance of power and prejudice was so overwhelmingly tilted in favour of the Europeans that periods of genuine coexistence were impossible.

In Mexico, European evangelisation was vigorous and successful. Cortés destroyed the great temple of Tenochtitlan in 1522 and had the new cathedral of Mexico built directly over it: what more graphic image could any Aztec need? But such a dramatic gesture seems less important than the thoroughness of the missionary follow-through during the first generation of conquest. By 1536 Mexico had a college to train Amerindians for the Catholic priesthood. By 1539, a short catechism in Spanish and Nahuatl was

98

printed in Mexico, the first in a long line of *Doctrinas* which eventually covered all the important native languages of Mexico and Guatemala. By 1555 Mexico had a dictionary of Nahuatl and Spanish. Ten years later came the first question-and-answer confessor's manual in Nahuatl – a good sign of a population well-organised into Catholic parishes. By then, the experiment of training an Amerindian clergy had been judged a failure, but the Mexicans had acquired something even more valuable for their subsequent religious history – the Virgin of Guadelupe, patroness of Mexican Indians, who first appeared to a converted Indian named Juan Diego within a decade of Cortés' conquest. Her cult (which absorbed features from a major Aztec goddess) was immensely popular among the Indians from the outset, and flourished despite the opposition of Mexico's missionary friars; to this day it remains the best-known shrine in the Americas. The Franciscans and their allies – about 800 monks in all of New Spain by 1559 – accomplished the religious conquest of Mexico before the Jesuits arrived in 1566. By then the *padres* had taken as firm a control of the religious life of millions of Mexicans as the few hundred *conquistadores* had of Montezuma's empire.[1]

This rapid and brilliant success was not repeated in the other major part of Spanish America. If Cortés had ceremoniously knelt in front of the 'twelve apostles', the friars whom he had specifically requested from Spain, Pizarro brushed aside a friar urging the importance of conversion with the remark that 'I have not come here for any such reasons; I have come to take their gold away from them.' Cortés destroyed major temples; Pizarro was content to loot them. And the consequences were different. Instead of a Virgin of Guadelupe, Peru had an important nativist religious revolt by the late 1560s. Elaborate *visitas* were carried out afterwards to destroy Inca idols and humiliate anti-Christian activists. Similar combinations of lashings and sermons were needed again after 1610, and after 1645. (The persistence of widespread 'idolatry' after more than a century of official Christianisation is reminiscent of the stubborn Catholicism in the seventeenth-century Pays de Vaud.) Peru's missionaries were less well-equipped than Mexico's: the second book printed in the colony was a *Doctrina* in Spanish, Quechua and Aymara, but it only appeared in 1584, and there were no grammars of a native language available until the seventeenth century. But at least Peru was better-off than Brazil, which permitted no printers in the colony until 1808, and whose most ambitious *Doctrina*, over a hundred pages long, was written in 1709 by French Franciscans.[2]

By 1600 Jesuits were the vanguard of missionary work in most parts of Catholic America. Their evangelisation laid the groundwork for a durable Catholicism in many places from Canada to the curious Indian republic they controlled in Paraguay. Though their reports have provided much valuable material for ethnographers, the Jesuits were not admirers of Amerindian religions in the same way as Bartolomé de las Casas, the much-studied sixteenth-century Franciscan champion of Indian rights. José Acosta, one of the best-informed Jesuit missionaries with long experience in Peru, and author of the widely-read *Natural and Moral History of the Indies* (Seville, 1590), was convinced that the many remarkable similarities between Inca and Castilian religious practices (fasting, convents of taboo women, confession, baptism, even doctrines resembling the Trinity) were not signs of ancient evangelisation, but rather the work of the Devil, the ape of God, who counterfeited genuine rituals in order to better deceive the Indians. Such resemblances, Acosta argued, may have facilitated the conversion of these peoples, but force was still sometimes necessary in order to complete the process:

although it is not permitted to force barbarian subjects into baptism and the Christian faith, it is licit and desirable to destroy their altars and temples and to banish their diabolical superstitions, things which are not only obstacles to the grace of the Gospel but also contrary to natural law.

If this was the language of one of the most accommodating Jesuit missionaries, one can imagine their general tone. Conversion of the Amerindians did not involve dogmatic compromises with essential tenets of indigenous religions, such as those made by other seventeenth-century Jesuits labouring in India or China.[3]

The pattern of Jesuit activities in the seventeenth-century Americas contrasts dramatically with the utter reluctance of Protestant powers to engage in serious missionary work when they entered the scramble for American colonies in the early 1600s. Ninety years after the foundation of Jamestown, a governor of Virginia blandly wrote home that 'no endeavours to convert the Indians to Christianity have ever been heard of'. The colony's lone famous convert, Pocohantas, was trying to raise funds for an

Indian college when she died, but no such institution was actually created in North America before the foundation of what is now Dartmouth College in 1769. There was exactly one famous Puritan apostle to the Indians, whose work was rubbed out by the uprising known as King Philip's War (1675–6), just as the earlier attack in Virginia (1624) had ruined the colonists' evangelistic impulses. Nor were the Dutch any more active than the English. 'We can say but little of the conversion of the heathens or Indians here, and see no way to accomplish it, unless they are subdued by the numbers and power of our people,' wrote two Calvinist *predikants* from the New Netherlands in 1657. The Dutch did a bit more during their occupation of Brazil (1624–54), printing a catechism in Tupi and sending some Tupi youths to Europe to learn civility and true religion. But the Dutch West India Company held only one piece of American territory for a long time and, as C.R. Boxer observed, 'about the progress, or lack of progress, of Calvinism in Surinam and the Dutch West Indian colonies during the seventeenth and eighteenth centuries, perhaps the less said the better.'[4]

He added that the clergy of the New Netherlands spent more time and energy in combatting Protestant dissenters than in converting Amerindians. Certainly, the same can be said even more loudly about the Calvinist clergy of New England. The story of religious pluralism in British America was an intra-Protestant affair for the most part. The founding – and survival – of a colony dedicated to complete and unrestricted religious freedom in 1636 was a unique event in the Christian world; the persecution of Quakers and other dissidents by Massachusetts Bay authorities is a far more ordinary and depressing aspect of seventeenth-century religious history. This subject has been well treated elsewhere, and need not detain us here, except to underline that religious persecution, as well as religious liberty, existed in New England in dimensions proportionately stronger than in England itself.

Many of these observations about religious coexistence can also be applied to the history of witchcraft in the Americas. The various colonists carried their fears of *maleficia* and witches among other items in their cultural baggage, as a sixteenth-century Peruvian chronicler recognised when he remarked that the Devil had arrived in the West Indies in some Castilian ship.[5] The colonisation of the Americas coincided with the major phase of European witch trials. The *Malleus Maleficarum* preceded Columbus's first voyage by just five years, and Spain's most famous play about a witch, *La Celestina*, coincided with his last voyage. Long afterwards, Champlain founded New France while DeLancre was launching France's greatest provincial witch-hunt, and James I composed his *Demonology* only ten years before chartering the Virginia Company. We should also remember that witch beliefs varied considerably from one colonising country to another. As we have seen, the Spanish Inquisition regarded witchcraft as a form of superstition, treated it leniently, and saw many more trials of sorcerers (*hechiceros*) than of witches (*brujas*). England had a remarkably slow development of diabolism and witches' Sabbats, while France gave an unusually important role to demonic possession and show trials in its witchcraft.

Given such national differences, and the varying degrees of missionary impulses among these colonising powers, it seems reasonable to expect that the history of witchcraft in the Americas would be different for each of the colonising powers, with each one resembling its own metropole, especially in so far as it was an internal event among colonists. But in another way witchcraft in the Americas was part of the acculturation of the Amerindians to Christianity – or of the acculturation of the African slaves, who increasingly peopled the West Indies and the Americas after the mid-sixteenth century. Since both the native 'Indian' and the transplanted African were culturally equipped with their own forms of magic and sorcery (though without the Devil who arrived in those Castilian or Protestant ships), their interaction with the European colonists whom they served provides a truly 'colonial' dimension to superstition in the Americas. For various reasons, the history of this acculturation varied greatly from place to place, and is often extremely difficult to reconstruct, although a few valuable clues can be found in anthropological literature.

Witchcraft in New and Old Spain was connected by the presence of the same institution on both sides of the Atlantic – the Inquisition – which Philip II established in both his American viceroyalties in the 1570s, and even introduced briefly into Brazil after becoming King of Portugal. The American Inquisitions, completed by a third tribunal at Cartagena in 1610, were 'colonial' organs, minutely supervised by the Spanish *Suprema*. Annual *relaciones de causas* were sent regularly across the Atlantic, and in the case of Cartagena the only surviving trial records exist in Spain.

Nearly everything we know about colonial witchcraft throughout Spanish America comes from Inquisitorial records, which are reasonably well-preserved, but incomplete because they had little to do with controlling the magical or idolatrous practices of baptised Amerindians or Africans. As early as 1575 Philip II ruled that the Indians were not *gente de razón* as were American-born creoles or half-castes (*mestizos*) and should thus be exempted from Inquisitorial jurisdiction. In Peru, where native 'idolatry' took so long to uproot, a special eccesiastical tribunal operated against Indian *hechiceros* into the eighteenth century, condemning several of them to lashings and even to the galleys. As in metropolitan Spain, the American Inquisitions were primarily concerned with eliminating crypto-Judaism and other heresies among the European settlers, as the *relaciones de causas* testify:[6]

Table 6.1   *American Inquisitorial cases, 1570–1700*

Tribunal (years)	Jews (killed)	Prots	Magic	Others	Total
Mexico (1571–1614)	123 (14)	95	35	546	799
Lima (1570–1614)	78 (12)	47	50	595	770
Mexico (1615–99)	35 (3)	2	38	176	251
Lima (1615–1699)	145 (18)	10	69	180	404
Cartagena (1610–99)	70 (3)	61	264	304	699

As in Spain, much of their routine business consisted of chastising morals offenders (bigamists slightly outnumbered Judaisers in colonial *autos*), blasphemers, and other non-heretical business.

Given such limitations, it is not surprising if the patterns of superstition revealed by these records seem similar in Castile and America, with a 'Mediterranean' emphasis on love-magic and similar forms of *hechicería*, but very few collective rituals of *brujería*. Of course, American Inquisitors were as obsessed as their Spanish counterparts with diabolical pacts and the element of apostasy in all forms of magical activity. Let us examine the work of the Lima Inquisition from 1625 to 1750 with a meticulous guide, José Toribio Medina. Over this century and a quarter, following an edict of 1629 which greatly increased the punishment of sorcerers and other magicians, more than a hundred *hechiceros* were investigated and sentenced at Lima. Between 1625 and 1666, Lima held seven *autos da fé* at which 168 people were sentenced; exactly a sixth of them were women condemned for *hechicería*, whereas at later *autos*, like 1693, almost half the victims were *superstitiosos* or *hechicerías*. Only one of Lima's first three dozen such suspects was male, a youth of nineteen accused of making a pact with the Devil who went unpunished because he was a 'mere prestdigitator'. Over the entire span, however, twenty-two of Lima's 103 witchcraft suspects were men and after 1700 men comprised nearly half of all suspects. At least four monks made some sort of pact with the Devil; several men (*curanderos*) used healing magic; one defrocked Dominican, punished in 1736, described himself as a *doctor en malvida brujería*, and had gathered a circle of female disciples.[7]

Furthermore, the age distribution of these Lima witches resembled seventeenth-century Castile, where many *hechicerías* were young widows, wives whose husbands had abandoned them, or living in concubinage, procuresses *à la* Celestina. A sample of three dozen whose ages are known shows that only three were older than fifty, while twenty were younger than forty. With a median age in their thirties, Lima's *hechicerías* were unlike the wrinkled crones who formed the basic European stereotype – but then, dealers in love magic should not be too old or live alone. These colonial Celestinas used a pharmacopia that was quite different from their European cousins. Some relied on crudely sympathetic love-magic, like the lawyer's widow who mixed powder from a church altar with menstrual blood and served it to men in cocoa. Several of them used other colonial products like canaries, or blended European recipes with colonial ones, such as prescribing either herbs picked on St John's Eve or tobacco juice as a nostrum against spells. A really avid client of these *hechicerías*, like the creole wife of a Cartagena official who tried alternately to tranquilise and stimulate her husband, employed a whole arsenal of magical nostrums, made from such things as asses' brains or the skulls of dead cats down to simple recipes including a broth made from a local grass and rubbed on the body, which is still in use. South America had much private sorcery, but little collective witchcraft. The only exceptions date from the eighteenth century, like the widowed *zamba* seamstress who sometimes 'joined together with other women on Thursdays and Fridays, flying at night in the shape of ducks . . . after saying *De viga en viga, sin Dios ni Santa Maria, lunes y martes y miercoles tres*'.

Another old widow was accused of virtually the entire gamut of European witchcraft – worshipping the Devil, damaging people and property through spells, causing sexual frigidity, predicting people's deaths, using magical wax figurines, and sacrificing live animals.[8]

At Cartagena, cases of *superstición* comprised 38 per cent of the Inquisition's business, by far the highest ratio anywhere in the entire Spanish system. The earliest *autos* described collective sorcery being practised by *cofradías*, and involving such serious crimes as poisoning. According to a mulatto surgeon, more than one *cofradía* functioned in Cartagena in the 1620s. They seem to have been real gatherings worshipping a pagan deity, managed by the god's *madrina* (a sort of queen-assistant), involving the distribution of private spirits to all initiates as well as the usual European details of renouncing the Christian God, baptism, and the Virgin, the *osculum infame*, the Devil's mark, ointments for flying, trampling on crucifixes, a goat-devil, and candlelight dancing. Cartagena's most prestigious *cofradía* was run by an African slave, who had a mulatto assistant, but otherwise admitted only creole initiates, including a student *presbítero* who was very useful for performing Christian sacrileges. The racial composition of her *cofradía*, plus the existence of mulatto *brujos* in Cartagena, illustrate the fact that many of the witches' clients and several of the initiates were creoles, but the key suspects were usually mulattos or African slaves. The Lima *hechiceros* included at least thirty mulattos or *mestizos* and fifteen African slaves among a hundred suspects, and this percentage might be even higher if we had more complete information about them.[9]

The Inquisitions were only concerned with magical practices which reached into creole society. We can hear the complaints of an Inquisitor in Quito in 1625 about the 'many superstitions and enchantments' there which resulted from too much interaction between creoles and Indians – complaints echoed by his successors in 1703 and 1706. It was even possible for the husband of a creole suspect in Cartagena to have her 'frequent use of herbs, powders and spells' for magical purposes absolved by the Inquisition largely on the grounds that she had been an orphan raised by Indians, and thus could not avoid sharing many of their superstitions. More rarely, creoles adopted non-European magic; an early eighteenth-century cleric in minor Orders told his confessor about his pact with the Devil, whom he addressed as *Señor del Africa*, and saluted with a raised first clenching some coca leaves. If Spanish historians argue that colonial American witchcraft was 'fundamentally native to Spain', this is an optical illusion arising from the fact that the Inquisition was fundamentally native to Spain and the people most affected by it were creoles or *mestizos*.[10] We still know too little about possible syncretisms among Indian, African, and European magic in Spanish America.

Mexico had a great many cases of sorcery and witchcraft that were settled locally and not reported in the *relaciones* sent to Spain – nine volumes just from 1580–1600, from which only two dozen names ever reached the *Suprema*. Pacts with the Devil came early: in 1601 a *mestizo* youth received 200 lashes and five years in the galleys for this reason. Yucatan had its *cofradías* like Cartagena. By 1619 the use of peyote for divination had become widespread among Mexican creoles. Although it displayed many of the same syncretistic features as South American superstition cases, sorcery in the more thoroughly Christianised soil of New Spain also eventually acquired the handbook or *grimoire* which appears to play a crucial role in contemporary Mexican magic.[11]

The other Catholic regions of colonial America, Canada and Brazil, possessed no established Inquisitions. Consequently, the source materials for their sorcery and superstitious syncretisms are more scattered and fragmentary. The basic work on witchcraft in Canada lists only three dozen accusations scattered between 1645 and 1830, mostly in the towns of Quebec or Montréal. Nobody was ever executed for witchcraft in New France, even before France herself effectively abolished the death penalty for witches in 1682. Few were even menaced with banishment, like the woman innkeeper at Montrèal who owned a book of magic. The kinds of sorcery which agitated Canadians were typically French, beginning with magical ligatures for sexual impotence, and peaking after 1725 with a crisis of demonic possessions – a problem which had ended in France with the Cadière case in 1717. Overall, Canadian punishments for witchcraft were remarkably mild, partly because in Canada, unlike France, this type of crime remained under ecclesiastical jurisdiction and partly because the Canadian Church ignored the magical practices of its mixed-blood population, the *coureurs des bois*.[12]

Illicit magic in Brazil is a more extensive subject, but also far more complex to disentangle. Two major problems hamper research: first, available sources on colonial superstitions are few because there was little Inquisitorial activity in Brazil, and because the Portuguese Inquisition was rarely concerned with sorcery, at least before the eighteenth century; secondly, Brazil's racial mixtures have continued to produce magical syncretisms right up to the present, making even regressive anthropology difficult. When Inquisitors made flying trips to Brazil in 1594–5 and 1618, half of their business was done with Jews or sodomites; only a few suspects were clients of witches, and only one was definitely a practising sorceress who had been banished from Portugal for this offence. On the other hand, north-eastern Brazil possesses one of the most vigorous survivals of non-European magical practices to be found anywhere in the Americas. Anyone who has seen a *candomblé* ceremony in Bahia need not read widely in order to appreciate the extent to which Brazil's Africans have created interesting magical and religious hybrids with Christianity; but this Brazilian magic tells us very little about the history of sorcery in Brazil, and nothing about its connections with Portugal.[13]

Witchcraft in the English colonies was very unlike that in the Spanish colonies. England was the only Protestant power to establish a durable American empire during the seventeenth century, and her only serious rival, the Netherlands, had executed her last witch before chartering a West India Company. Furthermore, England's American colonies generally had much less metropolitan supervision than their Spanish counterparts, and certainly no Inquisitions. Finally, sorcery in the English colonies was unique because only here were colonists put to death for witchcraft during the seventeenth century – eleven people in Connecticut and over two dozen in Massachusetts Bay, most of them in the Salem panic of 1692. For all these reasons, but especially the last one, New England's witchcraft is deservedly famous.

Studying the Salem witch panic has long been a minor American industry. Kittredge, one of its most capable practitioners, set down his major conclusions over fifty years ago, and some of them deserve repetition: New England's witch beliefs were brought over from the mother country by the first settlers; trials for witchcraft, and one death sentence, occurred in England after they had ended in Massachusetts; the public repentance and recantation of judge and jury in Massachusetts have no parallel in the history of witchcraft; 'the record of New England in the matter of witchcraft is highly creditable, when considered as a whole and from the comparative point of view'. Each point deserves a brief comment. The first is valid, and remains valid if we substitute 'New Spain' or 'New France' for New England, but the special mixture of beliefs brought over was specifically British, i.e. there were no orgiastic rituals to its Sabbats and the Devil's mark was the English extra nipple, rather than the continental anaesthetic scar. The second point is true but misleading, since it neglects to add that England saw no mass trials of witches like Salem's at such a late date. The third point is true and should be underlined: only a society as devout and as devoted to self-questioning as Puritan Massachusetts could admit its mistakes publically and in church. The final point is true only in a qualified way, since New England's record is not so creditable when compared with New Spain or New France.[14]

Although New England's witch beliefs were not radically different from those of seventeenth-century England, they did put more stress on the element of diabolical compact; when Massachusetts Bay decreed the death penalty for witches in 1641 or Connecticut in 1642, both underlined the enormity of 'fellowship with a familiar spirit' and cited Exodus to authorise their laws. Even more typical of Reformed attitudes was the fact that New England's witches had been forced by the Devil to sign a black book; only a 'people of the Book' could have created this form of apostasy. New England witchcraft included at least a few people who practised image magic. The first witch executed at Salem, Bridget Bishop, possessed 'several Poppets, made up of rags, and Hogs Brassels, with Headless Pins in them, the points being outwards' stuck in her cellar walls. New Englanders used such traditional British methods of divination as the sieve and shears, and they apparently liked to bury bottles holding the urine of bewitched persons or animals in order to afflict the witch. Unfortunately for the accused at Salem, New Englanders accepted spectral evidence at least as easily as the metropolitan British; and other colonists were still using the popular (although illegal) test of 'swimming' suspected witches as late as 1730.[15]

The New England Puritans were not the only British colonists who prosecuted witches. Bermuda had a serious outbreak as early as 1651, and Virginia had an interesting case as late as 1706. But it remains true that the epicentre of English colonial witchcraft was in Massachusetts Bay and Connecticut, not in the slaveholding and Anglican colonies to the south. Perhaps the contrast between the devout, Devil-fearing Puritans and the more easy going Anglicans, which has been obliterated by British witchcraft scholarship, still holds up in a colonial setting. And that colonial setting, even in New England where there was so little missionary work, was not exclusively English. The Salem panic began soon after the local minister's 'Indian man, and Woman, made a Cake of Rye Meal and the children's water, baked it in the Ashes, and gave it to a Dog, since when they have discovered, and seen particular persons hurting of Them.' The first person to be accused was a West Indian slave, apparently an authentic sorceress, whose husband, 'John Indian', soon proved himself one of the most adept diabolically-possessed accusers. Near the origins of the greatest Puritan witch-hunt were two Amerindians who adapted their folk magic to that of their masters in order to survive (which they both did, not being *gente de razón* and thereby escaping the full rigours of English law). Their interaction with the supposedly dominant colonial witch culture was less spectacular than Cartagena's *cofradías*, but equally significant.[16]

We still know little about non-European witchcraft in the colonial American empires, especially the sorcery of the native tribes. Most anthropological studies are unconcerned with the pace and extent of acculturation between European and American witchcraft, especially in the colonial era, and one of the few noteworthy exceptions seriously exaggerated the extent of Spanish influence on south-western American Indian witchcraft. What made European witchcraft unique was its blending of diabolism with sorcery, and very little diabolism can be found among the Navajos or their neighbours. Since sorcery, especially sympathetic magic, tends to be similar throughout the world, it seems difficult to prove any specific European influences on Amerindian witch beliefs.[17]

Perhaps even more interesting, and somewhat better studied, is the history of Afro-American witchcraft. Here one is dealing with exploited 'colonists', uprooted from Africa and forced into Christianity in a new environment. The forms of religious syncretism created under this kind of pressure naturally included a fund of syncretistic witch beliefs. Anthropologists tend to focus on Afro-American witchcraft in such places as north-eastern Brazil, where the slave trade lasted longest, and where the African element is thus proportionately less contaminated by Portuguese Catholicism. But for our purposes the most important form of Afro-American witchcraft is that practised in Haiti by adepts of the 'old religion' or *vodu*. Voodoo is a form of religion, not of witchcraft, although French colonists have confused the issue ever since the seventeenth century by referring to *vodu* priests as *sorciers*, in accordance with the Europeans' general mental shorthand of calling any pagan ritual 'witchcraft'. More precisely, *vodu* is the word for 'god' among the linguistically-related Fon tribes of Dahomey and Togoland, who comprised the majority of slaves sent to the French plantations of Saint-Domingue after its founding in 1660.[18]

What makes the history of Haitian *vodu* so relevant is not the purity of its rituals, but rather the richness of its syncretisms with Christianity, a richness made possible by the peculiar history of this colony. Until the 1790s, when the first serious ethnographer of *vodu* appeared, Saint Domingue's religious history was uneventful. Its arriving African slaves were baptised (sometimes more than once), but had no formal training in Christianity, despite the provisions of Louis XIV's *Code noir*. Thus they retained many 'Guinean' religious customs, including ritual nocturnal dances which colonial authorities had forbidden since 1704, beneath their Christian veneer. The remarkable aspect is that the *vodu* of contemporary Haiti does not differ too radically from the syncretisms described by Moreau de St-Méry in 1791. It has been preserved so well by Haiti's unique history: a successful black rebellion in 1795, which drove out the French and achieved independence by 1804. Haiti remained an Afro-American state, nominally Catholic, but not in communion with Rome until an 1860 concordat. No serious missionary drives disturbed its 'Guinean' *vodu* until the 1940s, and no new Africans have arrived since the 1780s to contaminate its relative 'Guinean' homogeneity. Thus, through a blend of independence, isolation, and benevolent neglect, Haiti long managed to retain an Afro-American (more precisely, Guinean-Catholic) religion in something like its eighteenth-century form, only without the French *colons*. (The persistence of Catholicism after independence had other parallels among Afro-Americans; one of the most impressive cases was the South American republic of the Esmeraldas, descended from ship-wrecked African slaves of the 1570s and Amerindian women, who fought the Spanish but sometimes welcomed Catholic priests.)[19]

Haitian *vodu*, like most other religions, has a place for sorcery and witchcraft. Because *vodu* is not African but syncretistic, it believes in the magical powers of the sacraments and therefore baptises its cult objects; it borrows much of its liturgy from Catholicism, except that Christmas rather than Easter is the peak of the *vodu* calendar; and it has partially assimilated the Christian saints. Thus it is not surprising to find both Guinean and Catholic elements in its beliefs about *bokos* or witches. A *boko* is frequently a priest (*houngan*) who 'uses both hands', i.e. who practises black as well as white magic. He can poison with *wanga* or even send a death-spell (*envoi-morts*): his most frightening power is to revive dead men in a state of near-idiocy and compel them to do his bidding (the *zombi*). All these beliefs are basically African, but Haitian witchcraft also has a Christian tinge (perhaps, as its ethnographer insists, because most contemporary *houngans* have read some French magical handbooks or *grimoires*). For instance, *zombi* will go berserk only if given salt, that taboo of the witches' Sabbat, and the best protective powders against witchcraft must be prepared on Christmas night. There may be European elements in the beliefs about *zobop*, rural witches who 'go out' at night in groups after being summoned by magical tambourines that only they can hear, who can metamorphose themselves into many kinds of animal, and who engage in nocturnal cannibalism; but they do not burlesque Catholic rituals at their gatherings, so the congruence with European Sabbats is incomplete. The most important gulf separating *vodu* from European styles of witchcraft is that *vodu* has no real counterpart to the Christian Devil. Apparently Legba-Petro, Lord of Crossroads, and Baron Samedi, Lord of Cemeteries, share most of Satan's powers between them. For example, *zobop* generally assemble either at a crossroads or in a cemetery, but only Baron Samedi can be invoked for a death-spell on humans or livestock.

Unfortunately very little is known about the history of Afro-American witchcraft beliefs in other cultural settings, but we can safely assume that it has been less well-preserved elsewhere since 1800, simply because other colonial slaveholders had more successful social controls and religious instruction by the nineteenth century. Even if the task of recovering other colonial Afro-American syncretisms of religion and magic seems impossible, the example of Haitian continuity with Saint Domingue testifies to the durable cultural interactions between slaveholders and slaves, confirming the lessons of the Cartagena *cofradías* or the origin of the Salem panic. The colonial Americas were a theatre for both the triumphant expansion of Christianity overseas and the fusion of European with foreign superstitions.

Notes

1 C.R. Boxer, *The Church Militant and Iberian Expansion 1440–1770* (Baltimore, 1978), 41–4, 15, 113, 69–70; Robert Ricard, *The Spiritual Conquest of Mexico* (Berkeley, 1966), 188–92; Jacques Lafaye, *Quetzalcoatl and Guadelupe* (Chicago, 1976).

2 Boxer, *Church Militant*, 41–4, 91, 114–15; Pierre Duviols, *La Lutte contre les religions autuchthones dans le Pérou colonial: 'L'extirpation de l'idolatrie' entre 1532 et 1660* (Lima-Paris, 1971).

3 Duviols, 68, 49; Boxer, *Church Militant*, 46–56.

4 W.F. Craven, *White, Red, and Black: The Seventeenth-Century Virginian* (Charlottesville, Va., 1971), ¯64, 32; Ola Winslow, *John Eliot, Apostle to the Indians* (Boston, 1968); C.R. Boxer, *The Dutch Seaborne Empire 1600–1800* (London, 1965), 149–52.

5 Duviols, 29 and n. 29.

6 Boxer, *Church Militant*, 85; Duviols, 217–26. The copious documentation from the Mexican Inquisition has been tabulated by Solange Behocaray-Alberro, *La actividad del Santo Oficio de la Inquisicion en Nueva España 1571–1700* (Mexico, 1981); also Manuel Tejado Fernandez, *Aspectos de la Vida social en Cartagena de Indias durante el Seiscientos* (Seville, 1954), 14–18, on Cartagena. This table, drawn from *relaciones de causas* (which in the case of Mexico and Lima cover fewer than half of all trials) is taken from an unpublished paper by Jaime Contreras.

7 José Toribio Medina, *Historia del Tribunal del Santo Oficio de la Inquisicion de Lima (1769–1820)*, 2 vols (Santiago, 1887), ii, 35–41, 257, 169–70, 300–1.

8 Ibid. ii, 176, 218–22, 234–5, 257, 296–8; Tejado Fernandez, 88–90. For the seventeenth-century Castilian Celestinas, see Sebas-

tien Cirac Estopañan, *Los proceses de hechicerías en la Inquisicíon de Castilla la Nueva* (*Tribunales de Toledo y Cuenca*) (Madrid, 1942), 214.

9   Tejado Fernandez, 108–140 *passim*, 307–23.

10 Toribio Medina, ii, 16–17, 214, 227–28; Tejado Fernandez, 75, 143.

11 These Mexican cases have been studied by Gonzalo Aguirre Beltran, *Medicina y Magia* (Mexico, 1963); see R.E. Greenleaf, *The Mexican Inquisition of the Sixteenth Century* (Albuquerque, 1969), 173–5, 188 n. 53, 224, for a brief introduction. William and Claudia Madsen, *A Guide to Mexican Witchcraft*, 5th edn (Mexico, 1979), offers clues about the current situation, and about the most common *grimoire*, the 'Book of St Cyprian'.

12 Robert Séguin, *La Sorcellerie au Canada français du XVIIe au XIXe siècle* (Montreal, 1961).

13 See Donald Warren Jr, 'Portuguese Roots of Brazilian Spiritualism', *Luso-Brazilian Review*, 5 (1968), 13, 30–1 and n. 93; and Patricia Aufderheide, 'True Confessions: the Inquisition and Social Attitudes in Brazil at the Turn of the 17th Century', ibid. 10 (1973), 208–40, esp. 234ff, By the eighteenth century, the most serious Brazilian offenders were taken to Lisbon for final sentencing.

14 George L. Kittredge, *Witchcraft in Old and New England* (New York, 1929), 373 (13, 15, 18, 20).

15 Ibid. 90, 102, 235–6, 274–5, 363–4; J.R. Taylor, *The Witchcraft Delusion in Colonial Connecticut, 1647–1697* (New York, 1908), 149–50. The problem of image magic in New England has been stressed (indeed, severely overstressed) by Chadwick Hansen, *Witchcraft at Salem* (New York, 1969).

16 Kittredge, 102–3, 358; the Virginia case was published by G.L. Burr, *Narratives of the Witchcraft Cases 1648–1706* (New York, 1914), 441–52.

17 Elsie Clews Parsons, 'Witchcraft among the Pueblos: Indian or Spanish?', *Man*, 27 (1927), 106–28. The best-known monographs are Clyde Kluckhohn, *Navajo Witchcraft* (Boston, 1944); and Beatrice Whiting, *Paiute Sorcery* (New York, 1950), to which the work of Aguirre Beltran (n. 10) should be added.

18 There is a large and often unreliable literature on Haitian *vodu*. A worthwhile introduction can be found in Melville Herskovits, *Life in a Haitian Village* (New York, 1936); the outstanding modern synthesis, on which this section is based, is Alfred Métraux, *Le Voudou haitien* (Paris, 1958).

19 John L. Phelan, *The Kingdom of Quito in the Seventeenth Century* (Madison, 1967), 3–22; other examples are in Boxer, *Church Militant*, 102–4.

7 THE ASSAULT ON SUPERSTITION, 1680–1725

'Superstition' has been a remarkably durable and highly flexible pejorative term ever since Cicero's day. It had different meanings for the pagan and Christian communities of Ancient Rome, just as it did on different sides of the confessional walls after the Reformation. Originally employed by élitist Romans, or their Greek admirers like Plutarch, to denigrate the religious practices of uneducated people, it was adapted by the Christians to ridicule the old Roman state religion, and by the medieval Church to condemn the 'barbarous' folk beliefs of northern Europeans. At the Reformation, Protestants turned the word against a great many Catholic practices unknown to the Scripture of which they disapproved. Reginald Scot, for example, quoted the Catholic definition of superstition as 'religion observed beyond measure, a religion practised with evil and imperfect circumstances; whoever usurps the name of religion through human tradition, without the Pope's authority, is superstitious', and proceeded to show how Catholics violated their own precepts. As late as 1674, a Protestant pastor in Basel published a remarkably long (1107 pages), and excruciatingly dull *Magiologia, or Christian Warning against Superstition and Magic*. For their part, Catholics continued to use the term, but tended to confine it to popular errors, as in Pedro Ciruelo's *Treatise Condemning all Superstitions and Magical Practices* (1530; reprinted mid-seventeenth century).[1]

However, both the intensity and the extent of the literature attacking superstition increased between 1680 and 1725, during an age of triumphant confessionalism and retreating popular culture. The assault on 'superstition' – which in some ways began in 1670 with Spinoza's *Tractatus Theologico-Politicus*, a more radical work than most of those discussed here – permeated the Anglo-French-Dutch *République des letters*, and helped prepare the way for the

114

world of the Enlightened. It was accompanied by a silent revolution which ended the execution of witches, and implicitly redefined witchcraft as superstition throughout western Europe, and by an even more silent refusal to burn 'sodomites' for heresy. All these phenomena were important aspects of the process which Paul Hazard identified as 'the crisis of European consciousness'.

The age of *sensibilité*, the age of scientific triumphs exemplified by the career of Newton, was also an age of triumphant confessional orthodoxies both Protestant and Catholic. Within the long-term history of Christianity, the late seventeenth and early eighteenth centuries seem a placid era, with few vital dogmatic quarrels. The great revolt of England's Puritans had gone down to defeat in 1660, leaving little to the dissidents beyond the literary glories of *Paradise Lost* or *Pilgrim's Progress*, both of which were completed not long afterwards. The great age of French Jansenism effectively ended with the 'Peace of the Church' in 1668, and its final literary glories came with Racine's last tragedies in the 1670s. Elsewhere, there appear to be no truly significant religious developments within Christendom until Pietism gained momentum in early eighteenth-century Germany, and no truly dangerous developments for established Churches until the rise of Methodism in England in the 1740s. Dissent either went underground or turned its energies to moralistic and educational writings. During the half-century after 1670, the state Churches of Christendom luxuriated in the mellow glow of an Indian summer, before their brutal confrontation with the corrosive religious relativism of the Enlightenment, announced by Montesquieu's *Persian Letters* in 1721. Until then, the triumph of confessional orthodoxies seemed complete within their respective spheres of establishment, and few of them were inclined to tolerate dissent. The most notorious action of this period, Louis xiv's revocation of the Edict of Nantes, was a diplomatic blunder, but a domestic success. It cost him the support of the German Protestants, prepared the way for his Dutch arch-enemy to become King of England, and even failed to end his quarrels with the Pope; but it remained the most popular act of his long reign with the 95 per cent of his subjects who were already Catholic in 1685.

Accompanying the triumphant confessionalism of the half-century after 1670 was an extremely sharp gulf between élite and popular culture throughout western Europe. Recent students disagree over whether this development was primarily due to state intervention, or whether it was caused by religious indoctrination and economic modernisation, but they agree that élite cutlure had moved further away from popular culture by 1750 than ever before. French historians tend to set the regime of Louis xiv, the epitome of classicism and absolutism, at the centre of this development: France promoted national legislation to segregate beggars, tried to eliminate both Catholic aberrations and Protestant worship, decriminalised witchcraft, and produced an official dictionary of its national language in 1694. It generally tried harder than other states to impose both order and cultural uniformity on its subjects, closeting away such unruly and disorderly elements as beggars and sorcerers. Not only was popular culture repressed or reformed, it was even preserved in forms suitable for the educated classes by two government officials, the Perrault brothers, who collected and edited the Mother Goose stories in the 1690s. Rarely was the division between dominant and unofficial culture so wide, and rarely was the latter so vigorously controlled, as in Louis xiv's France.[2]

Louis' omnipresent minister, Jean-Baptiste Colbert, intervened to overrule the condemnations of witches in three French provincial *parlements* in 1670–1, announcing a royal regulation on the subject which actually appeared over a decade later. It had been delayed by a famous cluster of trials before a special Parisian court, the *Chambre de l'Arsenal*, between 1676 and 1681; they involved investigations of more than a hundred people (including some prominent courtiers) and executions of nearly twenty underworld figures. Known as the 'affair of the poisons', these trials produced a series of charges including much diabolism and Satanism. In fact they offer the earliest reliable documentation in European history for the celebration of an authentic Black Mass, replete with defrocked priests and sacrilegious altars. In 1682 Louis xiv's government promulgated an edict which effectively decriminalised witchcraft. As Mandrou has pointed out, this law was relatively terse, did not result from prolonged deliberations, spoke mainly about poisoners (who had been so prominent in the *Arsenal* trials), and left few traces in contemporary pamphlets or other polemical literature. One of France's most conservative regional courts subsequently claimed that this edict 'contained at bottom nothing which did not conform to the true idea which the *parlement* of Rouen had concerning the crime of witchcraft [*sortilège*] and the punishment it deserved'. These legal changes may have signalled a profound crisis of conscience and the triumph of a new way of thought; but to conservative minds, in the British Isles as well as in France, there were never any revolutionary changes as the sin of witchcraft gave way to the crime of fraud or poisoning. It is truly ironic that the same government that quashed witchcraft indictments in 1682 was simultaneously implementing the violent policy of *dragonnades* against its religious dissidents: France registered major victories against superstition and against religious toleration in the name of absolutism.[3]

Condemnations of witches had ended in most parts of western Europe by the 1670s. Throughout the patchwork of French-speaking Protestant and Catholic states bordering the Jura mountains, the last important clusters of trials occurred in the 1600s, followed by a few isolated trials until the early 1680s. The same holds true for the larger patchwork of Lutheran and Catholic territories in south-western Germany examined by Midelfort, and in the equal-sized group of north German states studied by Schormann: the final set of witch panics in the 1660s, last sporadic individual accusations in the early 1680s. In the British Isles, the long list of assize session witchcraft indictments for the County of Essex ended in 1675, after a final outburst of five cases in 1670. Even in witch-ridden Scotland, where two legal executions took place in the Highlands as late as 1707, there were no serious outbreaks in the Lowlands after 1678–9.[4]

The effective end of witchcraft trials in western Europe around 1680 seems a silent revolution, where the innovators seldom explained their reasons. But it was far more self-conscious than the process which gradually ended another type of burnings at the stake in western Europe, the martyrdom of homosexuals or 'sodomites'. In Switzerland such burnings apparently ended about the same time as executions of witches: a decade earlier at Fribourg, a decade later at Geneva. Western Europe's most prestigious court, the *Parlement* of Paris, continued to burn 'sodomites' for half a century after they stopped executing witches in 1640. After 1700, as Michel Foucault has noted, the Parisian police investigated about 4000 suspected homosexuals, but almost never gave them worse punishments than imprisonment or banishment. 'One has the impression', he observes, 'that sodomy, formerly condemned under the same rubric as magic or heresy and in the same context of religious profanation, is now condemned only for moral reasons.' 'Sodomites' had indeed been condemned for just such reasons. A French jurist had argued in the 1550s that 'this sin ranks among the most execrable, prohibited by both divine and human laws, such that the Lord showed the rigour of his judgement by burning five cities for it'; a German jurist had explained in 1629 that across southern Germany, from Austria to Alsace, 'such a monster [*unmensch*] is called a heretic, and generally punished as a heretic, by fire'. The same punishment was, of course, meted out to witches on account of their apostasy to the Devil. In the Mediterranean world, sodomites were judged by Inquisitors rather than secular courts (at least in Aragon and Portugal) for such reasons. (One of the most intriguing differences between northern and Inquisitorial Europe during the seventeenth century was that the former – both Protestant and Catholic areas – burned witches and sodomites at the stake, but had stopped burning heretics, whereas the latter continued to burn heretics but not witches or sodomites. Neither development should be confused with the process of toleration or the elimination of superstition.) By the early eighteenth century, before the dawn of the Enlightenment but after the attack on superstitions by the Republic of Letters, even homosexuals were no longer burned at the stake as heretics.[5]

The outstanding symbol of this generation, a man who first achieved notoriety for a wide-ranging attack on superstitious practices and followed it with the most thorough attack on religious intolerance yet printed in Europe, before reaching the pinnacle of his literary fame in the 1690s, was Pierre Bayle. His first important work, the *Various Thoughts ... on the Occasion of the Comet which appeared in December 1680* (1682), was neither the first nor the only attack on the idea that comets portended evil developments – more than fifteen works in Holland and Germany debated the meaning, if any, of this comet – but it was the broadest discussion of the more general religious climate which surrounded this issue. The first quarter of the book began with astrology, of which cometology is a sub-division, and wandered around to discussing such topics as superstitions associated with names, before concluding his demonstration that none of the twenty-six comets which had appeared in the previous forty-three years was a presage. Three-quarters of his work was devoted to philosophical demonstrations that comets or other miraculous events could have no possible religious significance. The most remarkable and notorious part of these '*Various Thoughts*' was devoted to a lengthy discussion of the paradox, adapted from Plutarch, that a wise God would prefer atheism to superstition. As Bayle said in the preface to his revised edition,

It is a much-disputed question whether irreligion or superstition is worse: it is agreed that they are the two vicious extremities between which piety is situated. . . . One must be careful that superstition not enter under the mask of piety and seduce the spirit of a man so that he becomes its puppet. . . . It can incite to crime not only without any remorse, but even by persuading that one is obeying God, so that it overcomes all barriers which Reason and natural sentiments of honesy oppose to the passions. There are no ravages which Superstition does not commit in the heart and in the mind.

This philosophical defence of atheism was not the only reason that the book appeared anonymously, though it was probably the most important one.[6]

Bayle's greatest and most famous attack on religious intolerance appeared only four years later, immediately after the revocation of the Edict of Nantes, purporting to be a translation from the Elizabethan martyrologist John Foxe: *Philosophical Commentary on the words of Jesus Christ, 'Compel them to come in,' wherein it is proved by several arguments that nothing is more abominable than to make conversions by force, and wherein the sophisms of the converters by constraint are refuted along with the defence that St Augustine made for persecution.* The title accurately identifies Bayle's ultimate target, Augustine, and the attribution to Foxe, who favoured some toleration even for the Catholics who had burned so many of his Protestant martyrs during Queen Mary's reign, was well-chosen. But Bayle, with his love of paradoxes and tendency to follow lines of philosophical argument to their ultimate logical conclusions, surpassed Foxe and other previous theorists of toleration just as he had made the most daring attack on superstition by comparing it unfavourably to atheism. In this context, Bayle expanded the limits of religious toleration beyond toleration for Catholics (which few of his fellow Huguenots, especially those who like him had both a father and a brother killed during the 1685 persecutions, were prepared to admit) to include *all* religions. 'There can be no solid reason for tolerating any one sect, which does not equally hold for every other.' This rule applied to Jews, who had been omitted from nearly all Christian discussions of this problem, and to Mohammedans; it applied to the pagans who had been unjustly persecuted by the early Christian emperors. 'It is needless', Bayle added, 'to insist in particular for a toleration of Socinians, since it appears that pagans, Jews, and Turks have a right to it,' and he proceeded to roundly condemn the founder of the Reformed Church to which he proudly adhered for the death of Servetus. Bayle concluded with an eloquent general plea for the rights of the 'erring conscience'; it 'has to obtain for error the same prerogatives, protection, and indulgence [the French is *caresses*, which one could even translate as 'affection'] as the orthodox conscience obtains for truth'. Belief may be mistaken; but if it accords with the conscience of the believer it comes from God, and to force or oppose that conscience – so long as it does not disturb public order – is to commit a sin. Bayle's treatise, composed and printed in the land which had sheltered Spinoza, carried Dutch attitudes of *de facto* religious coexistence to their logical conclusions. It was scandalously in advance of its time: another century had to pass by before the American and French Revolutions would begin to write legal guarantees for the rights of the 'erring conscience'.[7]

Bayle was a resolute foe of superstition, but his position on witchcraft was considerably less novel and daring than his attitudes about atheism or toleration. His treatment of the subject occurred in his final farrago, the *Réponse aux questions d'un provincial* (1704), and seemed to hover between two different approaches. The relativist and Cartesian in him explained demonic possession as the result of a 'disordered imagination', sketched out an historical account of the 'antiquity and progress of magic', or jocularly suggested that such sorcery-ridden regions as Germany 'need a congregation *de propaganda incredulitate*, at least as badly as Japan and China have need of a congregation *de propaganda fide*'. But he also had to admit that there were true demoniacs, 'since Scripture does not allow us to doubt it', and even argued that 'true sorcerers, those who really have a pact with the Devil', deserve severe punishment because 'they sin against their conscience, renouncing voluntarily and knowingly the service of the true God'. With a typically Baylian paradox, he claimed that even if Spinoza, 'who did not believe in God or Devil', were a magistrate, he could not refuse to punish a guilty magician, because such people did not benefit from the rights of the 'erring conscience'. Real Calvinists always agreed that witchcraft was *not* superstition.[8]

Bayle was not a clergyman, although his father and brother were; he became a professor of philosophy and a journalist because of a weak voice. But it is significant that so many prominent figures in the 1680–1725 assault on superstition were clergymen. On the Reformed side, the most prolific author was the Dutch pastor Balthasar Bekker, who like Bayle began his career by opposing the idea that the comet of 1680 portended something evil. (It should not be forgotten that the annual fast day of the Swiss Reformed Church was devoted in 1681 to meditation on the consequences of this comet.) Bekker's most elaborate and best-known work was a four-volume frontal attack on all aspects of witchcraft, *De Betoverde Weereld* or 'Enchanted World' (1690–2). The book spawned over a hundred Dutch pamphlets during the next decade – overwhelmingly refutations; the author was solemnly defrocked from the ministry in 1692, while his book was being translated into the major languages of the Republic of Letters. Even if one agrees with Trevor-Roper's assessment that Bekker's work was virtually forgotten within fifteen years, the sheer scale of his attempt to compose a *summa* against witchcraft as a superstition deserves acknowledgement as the most comprehensive effort of its kind to be undertaken anywhere during the seventeenth or eighteenth century. His fate stands in curious counterpoint to that of the Anglican parson who composed his country's most thorough *Historical Essay on Witchcraft* (1718; enlarged edn, 1720). Whereas Bekker, living in a country which had executed no witches for a century, was hounded from the ministry, Francis Hutchinson, living in a land where witchcraft was still a capital crime, ended his career as a bishop.[9]

The writings of two French clerics, Jean-Baptiste Thiers and Pierre Lebrun, form an interesting comparison with Bekker and Hutchinson. Thiers, a parish priest from the diocese of Chartres, left a literary corpus whose titles illustrate the range of Catholic reforms under Louis XIV. They included, *inter alia*, a work on reducing the number of holy days (1668), soon put on the Roman Index; a treatise opposing the practice of exposing the Host at the altar (1673); a sizeable work, the *Treatise on Superstitions according to Holy Scripture, Conciliar decrees, and the sentiments of Church Fathers*

and Theologians (1679); a book on the strict enclosure of nuns
(1681); on prohibited and forbidden games and diversions (1686);
on whether or not priests should wear wigs (1690); on whether
monks or canons could grant Absolution to heretics (1695). His
Treatise on Superstitions was reprinted in 1697, enormously enlarged
by three volumes on *Superstitions which concern all the Sacraments.*
Like his early work on holy days, this book was censured by
episcopal decree in 1702. That year saw Thiers' final effort, two
volumes on *The most solid . . . of all devotions*, which was to follow
the commandments of God and the Church. He was an unusually
articulate member of the Jansenist clergy who attempted the
Herculean task of training their parishioners to accept a purified
Catholicism shorn of superstitions, but never of canonically-
approved practices.[10]

Theirs began his treatise on superstitions by harshly affirming
that 'whoever says superstition necessarily says pact with the
Devil', but his general guidelines for determining whether or not
something was superstitious seem less drastic. He proposed four
rules (I, c. 9):

1. Something is superstitious or illicit when it is accompanied by
   circumstances which are known to have no natural ability to produce
   the desired results (see Aquinas).

2. Something is superstitious and illicit when its expected results cannot
   reasonably be attributed either to God or to Nature.

3. Something is superstitious when the effects it produces cannot be
   attributed to Nature, and when it has been instituted neither by God
   nor directly by the Church to produce them.

4. Something is superstitious when it is performed by virtue of a tacit or
   explicit pact with Demons.

Much of this book, like Thiers' other polemics, consisted of an
elaborate compilation of ecclesiastical authorities, identifying
certain practices as superstitious, and arguing that the perpetrators
should be left to ecclesiastical justice because of the enormity of the
sins involved. Ultimately, as Thiers' title suggested, only the
Church could define what was and was not superstitious, and he
was acutely aware that such definitions had changed considerably
over time.

Of course not all superstitions were equally pernicious. Theirs
began with the most serious kind of 'false and superfluous cults',

including witchcraft and all forms of black magic as well as a wide range of other deviant religious practices, ranging from Judaism or Islam to the celebration of mass by an unordained person – precisely the sort of things which comprised the main business of Mediterranean Inquisitions. He borrowed examples from Calvin's treatise on relics, and cited St Charles Borromeo's burial of a false relic as the correct method for handling serious problems. Thiers' third book discussed divination, which was always a mortal sin and sometimes diabolically inspired. His final three books discuss less serious types of superstition, such as magical amulets or charms which involve no form of diabolical pacts either implicit or explicit. At the outset of Book IV, Thiers proposed two general rules for discerning superfluous practices, the milder type of superstition. One repeated his third rule from the earlier section – effects which surpass Nature but cannot be attributed to God, like the remission of mortal sins without the use of sacraments – but the other was new: practices whose results involve useless or ridiculous ceremonies instituted neither by God nor the Church, such as excessive flagellation. With the help of a network of ecclesiastical correspondents. Thiers had collected a long list of such practices, classified by the particular sacrament which was abused: the Eucharist had by far the longest entry, with baptism second. His lifelong patrol of the frontier between licit and illicit cults involved him in several heated literary quarrels, including one over the authenticity of the Holy Teardrop of Vendôme at the end of his life (1702).

His successor as a critic of superstitions, the Oratorian Pierre Lebrun, seems less radical. In 1693, Lebrun attacked the Cartesians' explanations of how divining rods work, and this essay became the point of departure for his unsigned *Critical History of Superstitious Practices* (1702). Like Thiers, Lebrun tried to demonstrate that 'only the successors of the Apostles can successfully oppose the progress of superstition', because they have a wider audience than laymen, and employ fewer sophistic arguments. Like Thiers, he collected many ancient and medieval texts, but shunned heretical authorities like Calvin. To Lebrun, superstition meant only excesses and disorders in divine worship. He pointed out that many non-malefic superstitions have been tolerated by Church and state alike. Lebrun carefully dissected practices connected with cults which contained abuses but also harmless and even beneficient elements: people are cured daily of snakebite in Auvergne by touching the tooth of St Amable and saying some prayers, all of which is done 'without any superstitious observances', just as St Hubert's relics really preserve people from rabies. Lebrun's hostility is directed towards practices like ordeals, a 'temptation of God', and especially against the swimming of accused witches. His final recommendations were simply to burn all books of magic, and require all sorcerers to repair the damages they had caused. Coming two decades after Colbert's witchcraft edict of 1682, Lebrun's essay seems like the timid beating of a dead horse.[11]

Catholic clerics played a central role in the attack on superstitions in Louis xiv's France. Some of them were prudently confined to internal memoranda, like the diocesan conference in Anjou in 1712 who took their entire agenda on superstitious practices directly from Thiers, naturally without naming him. Others preferred deeds, like the bishop eulogised by Voltaire as 'sufficiently enlightened to seize and have removed in 1702 a relic which had been preserved for several centuries and adored as the navel of Jesus Christ'. Although local notables launched a lawsuit against him, 'demanding the return of the sacred navel, the bishop's sober firmness at length prevailed over the credulity of the people'. Not all Catholic clergy were equally successful, however. When a French marquis converted to Lutheranism in 1711, largely because of the 'popular superstitions' he had seen in the Catholic Netherlands, an abbé tried unsuccessfully to reconvert him, blaming his failure on those ceremonies which 'mounted to such a degree of extravagance that I still doubt what I have read, seen, heard, and touched, since their absurdity seemed so incompatible with reason and so shocking to good sense.[12]

But if we seek Catholic priests who were much more radical and daring about superstitions than Thiers, we must go to Pietro Giannone of Naples, who published a *Civil History of the Kingdom of Naples* in 1723 which both ensured his fame and ruined his career. The principal theme of Giannone's *History* was the centuries-long struggle of Neapolitan monks to acquire much of their kingdom's wealth and political power; but the real scandal which caused him to flee Naples in 1724, fearing for his life, was his denial of the miraculous annual liquification of the blood of St Januarius. He fled to Vienna, where he lived for eleven years among the tiny freethinking entourage of Prince Eugene, and watched as his *History*, like Bekker's *Enchanted World*, was translated into the tongues of the Republic of Letters. It was certainly the most daring anti-clerical work to come out of Italy since Sarpi a century before, and it was even more congenial to Protestants and freethinkers because of its ironical attitude which discussed relics, holy images and pilgrimages merely as money-making practices. Ultimately, Giannone was expelled from Vienna and spent his final fourteen years as a prisoner of the Duke of Savoy, where he composed his other major work, the *Triregno*, which was not printed until 1895. Here, far from recanting, he argued that mankind would never attain the celestial or highest of these three kingdoms until the Church was destroyed – a vision worthy of a sixteenth-century Anabaptist. [13]

However, the most radical priest of all was French. Bekker had tried to demolish all forms of superstition; Giannone had created an economic interpretation of ecclesiastical history; but only Jean Meslier (†1729), a parish priest in the Ardennes, combined the economic interpretation of Christianity as exploitation of the poor by their rulers with the view that the Christian Church was itself a major form of superstition. His remarkable manifesto, *Mémoir of the Thoughts and Sentiments of J.M. on a part of the Errors and Abuses in the Conduct and Government of Men, where one may see clear and evident Demonstrations of the Vanity and Falsehood of all the Gods and all the Religions of the World*, probably composed about 1725, was the first truly atheist-communist treatise in the history of western civilisation. Its eighty chapters were evenly divided between five 'Proofs' of the falsehood of all religions, and one lengthy 'Proof' of how Christianity reinforced social injustice. [14]

Meslier's principal positions were sketched with relative brevity and clarity in his explanatory preface:

Disabuse yourselves, dear friends, of everything that pious ignoramuses or self-interested priests and doctors tell you and would have you believe, under the false pretext of their so-called holy and divine religion. You are as badly seduced and abused as anyone; you are every bit as much mistaken as the most benighted. Your religion is no less vain and no less superstitious than any other. It is no less false in its principles, no less ridiculous and absurd in its dogmas and maxims; you are no less idolatrous than those whom you call idolaters; the idols of the pagans differ from yours only in name and shape. In a word, everything that your

priests and doctors preach to you with such eloquence about the
grandeur, holiness and excellence of the mysteries they make you adore;
everything they tell you with such gravity about the certainty of their so-
called miracles, and everything they peddle with such zeal and confidence
about the wonderful heavenly rewards and the frightful punishments of
hell, are at bottom nothing but illusions, lies, errors, fictions, and
posturings, which were originally invented by sly politicians, continued
by seducers and impostors, received and blindly believed by crass and
ignorant yokels, and ultimately maintained by the authority of the great
men and sovereigns of the world, who have favoured these abuses,
errors, superstitions and impostures – who have even authorised them by
their laws – in order to hold ordinary men in thrall and make of them
whatever they wish.

Nothing in Meslier's uneventful biography explains his posthumous bombshell: he published nothing, and most of his known
correspondence was with a Jesuit. Perhaps only a rural priest could
commit the ultimate *trahison des clercs*, analysing the alliance of altar
and throne, anticipating Utopian socialism, or ranting about
hanging all rulers and all nobles after strangling them with the
entrails of priests.[15]
Meslier's manuscript was afterwards discovered by Voltaire,
who published an abbreviated and expurgated version with much
of the socialism omitted and with a Deistic prayer forged at the end
in order to reduce the shock effect of its communism and atheism.
Canonised in this fashion as a forerunner of the Enlightenment,
Meslier none the less sounded more radical in his hatred of clerical
posturings than the smooth-tongued *philosophes*. Basically self-
taught, a 'Spinoza in the wild state', Meslier reinforces the
argument that religious scepticism was bolder before the Enlightenment. Conditions were different by the time Voltaire sent
Meslier's emasculated writings to the printer. There was still an
occasional victim of superstition around, like the unfortunate
Bavarian nun executed for witchcraft in 1749, or more respectable
victims of religious intolerance like the Huguenot Calas or the
blasphemer La Barre on whose behalf Voltaire laboured. There was
also the Jew killed at Nancy in the same year as Calas (1761) for
desecrating the Host, or the Jesuit burned by the Portuguese
Inquisition that year for claiming that the Lisbon earthquate had
been a punishment from heaven, but about them the *philosophes*
maintained a discreet silence.[16] By and large, religious persecution

had become anachronistic, and 'superstition' see seemed to be in retreat on all fronts.

But many of these developments were simply the implementation, incomplete to be sure, of the assault on superstition and intolerance launched by intellectuals, often clerics, between 1680 and 1725. In words, it had moved from the deep religious impulses of a Bekker, Bayle, or Thiers to the sarcasms of a Giannone, a Toland, even a Meslier. In deeds, it had ended the mass persecution of witches in western Europe by 1680, and had almost ended the burnings of homosexuals for heresy by 1725. What truly dominated it was less the triumph of a scientific revolution, led by Newtonian physics, than the steady spread of Cartesianism through most parts of Christendom, from Giannone's Naples to Edinburgh. Without Cartesian rationalism and its mechanical universe, there would have been no viable alternative to 'superstition', no explanatory system which could permit the Republic of Letters to ventilate the 'crisis of European consciousness' without unduly disturbing the established confessions. Even so, Bekker was defrocked, Bayle deprived of his Chair of Philosophy, Thiers censured in both France and Rome, Giannone imprisoned. In the assault on superstition, the clerisy suffered casualties, but they were wounded rather than killed.

Notes

1 There is no satisfactory general survey of the concept of superstition; see D. Grodzynski, '"Superstitio"', *Revue des études anciennes*, 76 (1974), 36–60, for the period up to Justinian. Quote from Scot's *Discovery of Witchcraft*, Book xv, c. 24; also Lynn Thorndike, *A History of Magic and Experimental Science*, 8 vols (New York, 1923–58), viii, 571. Ciruelo's *Treatise* has been translated by E. Maio and D. Pearson (London, 1977).

2 Cf. Peter Burke, *Popular Culture in Early Modern Europe* (London, 1978), 234–86, with the 'statist' hypothesis of Robert Muchembled, *Culture populaire et culture des élites* (Paris, 1978); or Yves-Marie Bercé, *Fête et révolte* (Paris, 1976). On Mother Goose, see Marc Soriano, *Les Contes de Perrault, culture savante et traditions populaires* (Paris, 1968).

3 Robert Mandrou, *Magistrats et sorciers en France au XVIIe siècle* (Paris, 1968), 425–86 (quote, 483).

4   William Monter, *Witchcraft in France and Switzerland* (Ithaca, 1976),
    37; Erik Midelfort, *Witch-Hunting in Southwestern Germany
    1562–1684* (Stanford, 1972), 223–9; Gerhard Schormann,
    Hexenprozesse in Nordwestdeutschland (Hildesheim, 1977), 109; Alan
    Macfarlane, *Witchcraft in Tudor and Stuart England* (London, 1970),
    271; Christina Larner, *Enemies of God* (London, 1981), 77–8.

5   William Monter, 'Sodomy and Heresy in Early Modern
    Switzerland', *Journal of Homosexuality*, 6 (1981), 46, 48–50; F.
    Fleuret and L. Perceau ('Dr Lodovico Hernandez'), *Les Procès de
    sodomie en France (XVIᵉ–XVIIIᵉ siècles)* (Paris, 1920), 40–60 (ex-
    ecutions 1677–80), 88–190 (execution of Benjamin Deschauffours,
    1726, also guilty of murder); Michel Foucault, *Histoire de la folie à
    l'age classique* (Paris, 1960), 108–10 (quote, 109); Michel Rey, 'Du
    Pêché au desordre: police et sodomie à Paris au XVIIIᵉ siècle', *Revue
    d'histoire moderne et contemporaine*, 29 (1982), 113–24.

6   The major interpretation is by Elisabeth Labrousse, *Pierre Bayle*, 2
    vols (The Hague, 1963–4). Quote from Labrousse's short *Pierre
    Bayle et l'instrument critique* (Paris, 1965), 132; a chart of publications
    about comets between 1640 and 1720 is in Willem Frijhoff,
    'Prophétie et société dans les Provinces-Unies aux XVIIᵉ et XVIIIᵉ
    siècles', in *Prophètes et sorciers dans les Pays-Bas, XVIᵉ–XVIIIIᵉ siècle*
    (Paris, 1978), 274.

7   Translations from Howard Robinson, *Bayle the Skeptic* (New York,
    1931), 84; and from T. K. Rabb, 'The Study of Religious
    Toleration in Theory and Practice: Heretics and Jews in the Age of
    the Reformation', paper read at American Historical Association,
    Los Angeles, 1981, 15.

8   The best account is in Robinson, *Bayle the Skeptic*, 224–31.

9   H.R. Trevor-Roper, *Religion, the Reformation, and Social Change*
    (London, 1968), 173–4 and n. 4. Cf. Wallace Notestein, *A History of
    Witchcraft in England, 1558–1718* (Washington, 1911), 342–3, on
    Hutchinson.

10 See the article on Thiers in *Dictionnaire de théologie catholique*, xv, 618,
    for a bibliography which omits a few of his titles like his work on
    wigs, printed 'at the author's expense': Newberry Library, Chicago,
    W/945/872. See also Jean-M. Goulemet, 'Démons, merveilles et
    philosophie à l'Age classique', *Annales*, 35 (1980) 1223–50.

11 On Lebrun, see *Dictionnaire de théologie catholique*, ix, 102–3; quotes
    from his *Histoire critique des pratiques superstitieuses*, (Paris, 1702), ii,
    c. 1; iii, c. 4.

12 Francois Lebrun, *Les Hommes et la mort en Anjou aux XVIIᵉ et
    XVIIIᵉ siècles* (abridged edn, Paris, 1975), 296–7; Voltaire, *The Age
    of Louis XIV*, ch. 35, at end; Y.-M. Bercé, *Fête et révolte* (n. 4), 139.

13   See the sketch in Paul Hazard, *European Thought in the Eighteenth Century* (London, 1953), 66–72; for the Viennese group who sheltered him, see G. Ricuperati, 'Libertinismo e deismo a Vienna: Spinoza, Toland e il *Triregno*', *Rivista Storica Italiana*, 79 (1967), 628–95.

14   Maurice Dommanget, *Le Curé Meslier: Athée, communiste et révolutionnaire sous Louis XIV* (Paris, 1965).

15   Meslier, *Oeuvres complètes*, ed. Desne, Deprun, Soboul, 3 vols (Paris, 1970–2), I, 20, 23.

16   Cecil Roth, *A History of the Marranos*, 3d edn (London, 1958), 350; Alexander Hertzberg, *The French Enlightenment and the Jews* (New York, 1968), 34; David Bien, *The Calas Affair* (Princeton, 1960).

8 TOLERATION AND ITS DISCONTENTS IN EAST-CENTRAL EUROPE

Both the social history and the religious developments of east-central Europe were unique in the early modern era. Three large kingdoms – Poland, Bohemia, Hungary – marked the eastern frontier of Latin Christendom. The region as a whole differed from western or southern Europe because it participated fully in the 'second serfdom' which had begun in the later middle ages, and because it was far less densely populated, with few important cities. It had relatively weak central governments: the aristocracies of Poland, Bohemia and Hungary enjoyed privileges far beyond those of their western counterparts.

Moreover, the religious history of east-central Europe during the sixteenth and seventeenth centuries was as unique as its social or political history. During the 1500s this region was a showcase of religious coexistence. The kingdom of Poland boasted its Warsaw Confederation (1573) joining three Protestant groups and accepted by Catholics; the Bohemians had their Letter of Majesty (1609), capping a long development of confessional pluralism; while Hungary, trisected by Ottoman victories, saw a Diet in Transylvania recognise the legal equality of no fewer than four religious (Catholic, Lutheran, Calvinist, Unitarian) in 1570. Yet during the seventeenth century this same region became the showcase of Catholic reconquest. Finally, east-central Europe was a mixture of different ethnic enclaves – German, Slavic, Magyar, Jewish – where religious preferences were closely linked to ethnic and linguistic blocs. This essay will explore some of the stresses and accomodations which resulted from the interrelationships among these phenomena.

All three kingdoms underwent important political changes around 1525. In Poland, a Renaissance monarch with an Italian wife negotiated a treaty with the Teutonic Knights who controlled much of the Baltic region: Sigismund I recognised Albrecht of Hohenzollern, former Grand Master of the Knights, as his vassal in the capacity of Duke of Prussia. Although Sigismund led 8000 men to Danzig in 1526 to quell religious extremism in the great port city, he had no objection to accepting suzerainty over a Lutheran state (Prussia), or to permitting Lutheranism to remain the official religion of Hanseatic Danzig, where he executed factional leaders, but not Protestant clerics. In the east, Sigismund continued his predecessors' policy of personal but not institutional union with the Grand Duchy of Lithuania, a vast region inhabited mainly by Greek Orthodox nobility and peasants. (In the early 1500s, Poland-Lithuania contained about 3 million Catholics and 2 million Orthodox.) In Lithuania, the Orthodox nobility had enjoyed legal equality with Catholics since the 1430s, although they sat on the Grand-Ducal Council only by special permission – a restriction removed by Sigismund's successor in 1563, shortly before the fusion of these two states. Poland's capital, Cracow, boasted one of Christendom's finest universities (its alumni included Copernicus and Dr Faustus) and was the only town allowed to attend the Polish Diet, where its representative could vote, but not speak. The Kingdom of Poland was enjoying a cultural golden age, and was well on its way to becoming the 'Commonwealth of the Gentry', where the monarch lost constitutional initiative to the middling nobility, who in turn gained complete control over their serfs in order to manage the grain-exporting estates on which Polish prosperity depended.[1]

The Kingdom of Bohemia consisted of the 'incorporated lands' of Moravia, Silesia, and Lusatia in addition to Bohemia itself. Far smaller and more compact than either Poland or Hungary, it contained perhaps half the population of Poland-Lithuania. Each of its incorporated lands had independent representative assemblies, and the 'kingdom' as a whole had almost no common institutions. Silesia, largely Germanic with some Polish peasants, frequently affirmed its links to the Holy Roman Empire; Moravia and Bohemia, basically Czech with important German minorities, nearly always ignored such links. In 1526 the new King of Bohemia, by virtue of a crucial election which involved a dynastic change, was Archduke Ferdinand of Habsburg; he ruled Bohemia for forty years and began the long process of incorporating this kingdom into the Austrian Habsburg lands. The towns of this ramshackle kingdom seem slightly less impotent than in Poland, and the 'second serfdom' had not proceeded as far or as fast as in Poland (peasants were prohibited from appealing directly to the king only in 1558). But the most pertinent comparison is that in Bohemia proper, religious affairs were governed by the fifteenth-century Basel Compacts, which guaranteed freedom of worship and legal equality to both Catholics and Utraquists (the heirs of the Hussites) – a situation much like Lithuania's, but unlike anything in western Europe at the beginning of the Reformation.[2]

The King of Bohemia who Ferdinand succeeded was Louis Jagiello of Hungary, who was slain on the battlefield of Mohacs. Louis left his principal kingdom in far worse shape than Bohemia. (The union between these states had been less cordial than between Poland and Lithuania: when Louis requested Bohemian help against the Turks, he was told they would rather fight against the Magyars 'and wipe out this accursed people'.) Before Mohacs, the kingdom of Hungary had been a relatively unified state of almost 4 million with no religious problems comparable to those posed by Orthodox or Utraquists; its ethnic minorities (Slovaks, Croats, and the ubiquitous Germans) seemed ready to develop into a major European polity under Matthias Corvinus (†1490). But the battle of August 1526 changed all that, dividing Hungary into three roughly equal portions for the next century and a half. The western strip, from the Adriatic to the Polish border, went to Archduke Ferdinand along with the title of King of Hungary; the central and southern parts were annexed by the Turks and divided into four *vilayets*; while the eastern part became the autonomous Principality of Transylavania, a Christian state paying tribute to the Turks (but strictly forbidding all public worship by Moslems) in order to maintain its independence from Habsburg Vienna. Serfdom was further advanced in Hungary than in Bohemia, because of the brutal repression following the great peasant revolt of 1515.[3]

Transylvania, the most important part of Hungary for our purposes, had been governed since 1437 by the Union of Three Nations, a confederation among Hungarian nobles, the frontier settlers or Szekelers (organised 1473 into orders), and the Saxons (organised into seven districts, or *Siebenbürgen*). The only Hungarian prince to escape at Mohacs was the Transylvanian *voivode* John Zapolyai; chased into exile by the Saxons, he followed French advice in Poland and became an adopted son of Sultan

Suleinan in 1529, returning two years later to crush the Saxons with Szekeler and Romanian help. (It is worth noting that even Ferdinand of Habsburg also became an adopted son of Suleiman in 1533 in order to guarantee possession of *his* share of Hungary.) Adding to the ethnic and cultural pluralism of Transylvania was its religious confusion. The Saxons, like other Germanic elements in eastern Europe, quickly embraced Lutheranism and formed a 'national' Church which endured substantially unchanged until World War II. Most of the Hungarians embraced Calvinism shortly afterwards, and many of them were still Reformed in 1914. The Unitarian Church, which gained official toleration in 1570, still numbered 32,000 members in 1786 and kept its Academy in Koloszvar until the twentieth century. Although its numerous Greek Orthodox Vlachs or Romanians suffered more discrimination here than in Lithuania, they too retained a church hierarchy in Transylvania throughout the early modern era. And of course Catholicism never disappeared. In many ways sixteenth-century Transylvania was the logical extension and exaggeration of many religious developments common throughout east-central Europe.[4]

Over much of the sixteenth century, the religious climate of the entire region was sharply unfavourable towards Catholicism. Although the kings of Poland, Bohemia and Hungary remained Catholic, they could do little to stem the rapid growth of Protestantism among their nobles and burghers. As in Transylvania, the first wave was a rapid and massive adoption of Lutheranism among all parts of the German *diaspora* scattered from the Baltic to the Carpathians. Next came a surge of Calvinism among the Slavic and Magyar élites, although some Czechs and Slovaks preferred Lutheranism and some Poles and Magyars turned to more exotic forms of Protestant radicalism. In these lands of serfdom, public opinion meant noble opinion, and the stubborn conservatism of the region's peasants counted for even less than the traditionalism of the region's monarchs. The religion of the landlord, not the religion of the prince, mattered. Within this general picture, the most significant episodes in the history of toleration in sixteenth-century *Mitteleuropa* concern the acceptance of antitrinitarian or other extremists and local-level co-operation between Protestants and Catholics. A salient example from each kingdom should suffice.

Our earliest case is the treatment of the true heirs of radical Hussitism, the Bohemian Brethren, under Ferdinand I. In the 1530s they carefully eschewed such doctrines as pacifism or adult baptism in order to distinguish themselves from the German Anabaptists who had been outlawed by the Bohemian and Moravian Diets in 1534. None the less, one of their leading preachers was imprisoned in 1535, so they sent a delegation of nobles to Vienna in order to present the Brethren's confession of faith to Ferdinand and assure him of their loyalty. He reportedly told them, 'Believe what you want – but we will stop you from meeting together and carrying out your superstitions'. Ferdinand actually did little until 1548, when sixteen leaders of the Brethren were jailed and kept there until they converted to Utraquism. A general decree of exile or conversion to Utraquism followed; hundreds of families emigrated, and public assemblies of the Unity ceased by 1550. Meanwhile, Jan Augusta continued to direct the movement from within prison for many years. The clandestine wife of a Habsburg archduke, sequestered in the same castle as some of the Brethren's leaders, finally persuaded Ferdinand's officials to release Augusta and his faithful disciple-secretary in 1561. Both emerged to take baths and discuss religion with some Utraquists and Jesuits. When confronted with the requirement to convert to one of their religions, Augusta refused, and returned to prison; his secretary, who had turned Utraquist, took a job in the castle in order to remain near him. There they stayed while the history of the Unity continued – not only in Poland, where several prominent leaders found shelter, but also in Bohemia and Moravia. When the Brethren presented another confession of faith to Ferdinand's successor Maximilian in 1575 it was signed by more lords and knights than the one forty years before.[5]

The story of Franz David, founder of Transylvania's Unitarians and reputedly of its Sabbatarians, offers almost as many constraints. The son of a German shoemaker in a principal town (known to Germans as Klausenburg, to its mostly Hungarian sixteenth-century population as Koloszvar, and to today's mapmakers under its Romanian name of Cluj-Napoca), he was originally educated for the Catholic priesthood, but like so many key figures of his generation soon turned Protestant. David, who was bilingual but wrote mostly in Hungarian, came under the influence of Magyar Calvinists, and by 1565 had become the first

Reformed bishop (*superintendus*) of Transylvania and court preacher. His friendship with the physician to the young Zapolyai prince, none other than the antitrinitarian exile Giorgio Blandrata, soon turned him into a reader of Servetus; he and Blandrata collaborated on Transylvania's first major Unitarian work, *The True and False Knowledge of God* (1567). David shook off the patronage of Peter Miliusz, *superintendus* of Hungarian Calvinism, at a Transylvanian disputation in 1569. Soon he turned apocalyptic and began proclaiming the probable end of the world in 1570. What occurred instead was a new Catholic prince of Transylvania, Stephen Bathory, who deposed David but named a Calvinist as his chaplain and confirmed the rights of antitrinitarians along with the two other Protestant Churches. David continued as Koloszvar's leading preacher and was confirmed as Unitarian *superintendus* in 1576. He began to move beyond Blandrata, just as he had done with Miliusz. At the Synod of Torda, attended by 322 Unitarian clerics in 1578, David rejected both infant baptism and prayers to Christ. Next year, Bathory (now also King of Poland) began a trial against him, relying on Blandrata who had acknowledged the divinity of Christ. Condemned to house arrest, David died in 1579 as a Sabbatarian, refusing to worship on Sundays. The movement he started survived among Transylvania's third 'nation', the Szekelers, despite legislation against it by the Diet in 1595, 1601, 1610, 1618, 1622 and 1635. Finally came mass trials in 1639, when hundreds of Sabbatarians were condemned to forced labour – a persecution directed by Calvinists, who used them as a pretext for attacking Unitarians.[6]

Poland offers no tales of Catholic princes with Calvinist court preachers or quiet castles sheltering morganatic Habsburg wives and notorious arch-heretics. Here the most significant settings for *de facto* religious pluralism were cities, particularly the economically powerful towns on the Baltic or Vistula and the old Polish capital of Cracow. In the former, strongholds of Lutheranism since the 1520s, public worship by Catholics was never forbidden, but there was some informal discrimination against them. By the 1570s only three Catholic churches remained in Danzig, a city of 30,000, and in some key Prussian towns like Elbing there was none. In Torun, Copernicus's city, Catholics held four of eight churches, one of them shared with the Lutherans (both used the same choir). But in Cracow, no Protestant services

were permitted inside the city walls until the Polish branch of the
Czech Unity was granted this privilege in 1568. Cracow's
Protestants bought a town house in 1571 and converted it into a
church, with Calvinists using the ground floor and Lutherans the
first floor; a royal charter confirmed their rights in 1572, but
extended no such liberties to antitrinitarians. In 1574 this building
was ransacked by a Catholic mob which burned Protestant books.
Other harassment followed, until the church was destroyed in
1591 (because it was made of brick, it was burned down from
inside; the antitrinitarians' Cracow house, built of wood, was
dismantled in order to avoid a fire). Late in the century, Poland's
capital was moved to Warsaw, in a province with no Protestant
nobility. Although this city was the site of the famous
Confederation guaranteeing the civil rights of all Protestant
noblemen, it never had a Protestant church. When the building of
one was begun in 1581, a mob destroyed the half-finished building,
and scattered the construction materials.[7] In Poland, people were
almost never killed for religious reasons during the sixteenth
century, but buildings and books suffered much casual violence.

In one significant area, however, the religious currents of
sixteenth-century east-central Europe were marked less by
toleration than by cultural imperialism. Relations between
Orthodox Slavic subjects and Latin rulers, whether the Catholic
Grand Dukes of Lithuania or the mostly Protestant princes of
Transylvania, show a pattern in which conversion rather than
coexistence became the dominant mode. Of course, Protestants
and Catholics went about converting their Orthodox subjects in
different ways and with different degrees of success. The two most
significant attempts came in Transylvania, where Magyar
Calvinists tried to create a stong Protestant Church among the
Romanians, and in Poland-Lithuania, where the Jesuits laboured
to build a Ruthenian Church faithful to both Rome and Poland.

Transylvania's Saxons printed a Romanian and then a Greek
modification of Luther's catechism in 1544, proselytising in the
vernacular because the Romanian clergy used a liturgical language
(Old Church Slavonic) which was as incomprehensible to their
flocks as Latin was to Magyar peasants. A Protestant press
publishing in Romanian was active from 1559 to 1581; originally
Lutheran, it soon produced Calvinist works, including a copy of
Marot's Psalms translated from Magyar. By 1566, the

Transylvanian Diet required that Orthodox priests be examined on their knowledge of the Bible by a Protestant-leaning Romanian bishop. In 1567 he summoned a synod of Orthodox clergy and required them to hold their services in Romanian, thereby creating a Romanian Calvinist Church, while the Diet expelled all other Orthodox bishops. The Catholic riposte came under Prince Bathory, who created a new Romanian bishop for all of Transylvania in 1572, and persuaded the Diet to accept his diocese in 1579. The reaction of the Romanian clergy, who appreciated official recognition, was to develop an enduring distrust for all books in Romanian (especially since printers used a Latin rather than Cyrillic alphabet for their editions after 1572). In the 1600s, when Transylvania became a militant Protestant state, the Magyars re-established a Protestant Romanian bishop, insisted on the use of Romanian in the liturgy, and reopened a Romanian language press in 1638. This final missionary thrust included the creation of a Calvinist Academy in 1657 with one wing for Romanians and one wing for Hungarians, connected by a portico. After the Habsburgs took over Transylvania in the 1690s, the Romanian Protestant churches dwindled rapidly, although a few congregations survived until the 1720s.[8]

In the united kingdom of Poland-Lithuania (Union of Lublin, 1569) the first major development was the conversion of several prominent Ruthenian noblemen (who had received full civil equality with the 'Latins' in 1563) to Protestantism. Here too the first missionary impulses had come from German Lutheranism – more specifically from the new University of Königsberg (1544), which printed the first books in Ruthenian and welcomed the Lithuanian nobility who had mistrusted the Polish university at Cracow. By 1560, Lithuanian noblemen can be found at the University of Basel, and in 1562 the Polish Calvinist pastor Simon Budny published a 498-page catechism in Ruthenian, using Slavonic characters (all subsequent Calvinist propaganda in Lithuania was printed in Polish). Conversions were rapid. The secular magnates who sat in the Polish-Lithuanian Senate in 1572 included forty-five Poles and twenty-four Ruthenians. Among the Poles, twenty-five were Catholic and twenty-one were Protestant; among the Ruthenians, one was Catholic, fifteen were Protestant and only eight remained Orthodox. One understands why Polish Calvinists contemplated the creation of a university in the Lithuanian capital of Vilna in 1570 (the king forestalled them by founding a Jesuit college there that year) and why there were 190 Protestant churches in Lithuania in 1572, many of them in entirely Ruthenian regions bereft of Catholic parishes.

None the less, the Grand Duchy of Lithuania was also the scene of the earliest and most brilliant Catholic reconquest. The story of her most important Ruthenian magnate family, the Chodkiewicz, is paradigmatic. Its eldest branch remained Orthodox, but its cadet branch turned Calvinist around 1560; the son of the Calvinist, named Grand Marshal of Lithuania in 1568, publically converted to Catholicism in 1572 after hearing a disputation between a Calvinist and a Jesuit. The path to the Union of Brest (1596) is already visible. By 1606 the group of Ruthenian magnates in the Polish Senate included only one Orthodox, seven Protestants, and twenty-one Catholics.

The Union of Brest, which brought a sizeable fraction of the Ruthenian Church under Roman obedience, did not lead to the withering-away of the old Orthodox Church as its promoters had hoped, but it did prove a far more durable solution than the Romanian Protestant Church in Transylvania. The Uniate Church was beset with problems from both sides. Although it was ratified by the Polish Diet in 1597, its metropolitan was never permitted to sit in the Polish Senate alongside the Catholic bishops, despite several papal pleas. The prestige of Polish Catholicism, purveyed by Jesuits in numerous Lithuanian colleges (most Jesuits in Poland were working in Ruthenian zones in the early 1600s), seduced many magnates into turning Catholic rather than Uniate.

Meanwhile, the Patriarchs of Constantinople, deprived of Muscovy after the elevation of a Patriarch in Moscow in 1584, worked hard to keep the Ruthenes faithful. The Uniates never gained a foothold in south-eastern Poland-Lithuania, the Ukraine; in the north-east, at Plock, the Uniate archbishop was massacred by a mob in 1623; a philo-Protestant Metropolitan of Constantinople, Cyril Lucar, incited the Cossacks against them; their Metropolitan narrowly escaped assassination in 1609. Yet the Uniates survived, and by the 1660s outnumbered Catholics in the old lands of the Grand Duchy of Lithuania. Both the weak political position and the significant cultural impact of the hybrid Uniate

Church have been sympathetically summarised by a French scholar, who observed that:

At the time of the Union of Brest, only one Ruthenian bishop understood Latin. Their successors in the Union were educated at Rome. ...Latin became their theological language, so much that their leader Mohila submitted his *Confession of the Orthodox Faith* to the 1640 synod in Latin.... Mohila's influence in Russia was both strong and durable. His followers, despite sharp opposition, maintained dominance within the Russian Church until the reign of Catherine the Great, when they were replaced by German Lutherans.

The Uniate Church thus offered the closest approximation to a Polish occupation of Russia, and also provided a blueprint for subsequent negotiations between Jesuits and Orthodox clergy in the Habsburg lands.[9] Throughout east-central Europe there was widespread *de facto* toleration during the sixteenth century, with multiple forms of Protestantism. Yet, as Evans has observed, 'Protestantism stood vulnerable on three counts by 1600: it could appear divisive, unhistorical, and radical.... There is a very real sense in which the tide of history ran for Protestantism during the sixteenth century and against it thereafter'.[10] The Turkish scourge which had devastated a corrupt Church and state in the 1520s had not gone away after the worst abuses had been corrected. Whatever the underlying causes and whatever the pace of change, the seventeenth century proved disastrous for Protestantism in this region. All three kingdoms saw massive conversions to baroque, post-Tridentine Catholicism, but the modalities of these changes were vastly different. In Poland the shift came early, was accomplished without religious warfare, and marked only a gradual break with local customs of peaceful coexistence; Polish historians can still speak with pride about religious toleration in the 'silver age' between 1600 and 1650. In Bohemia it was precisely the reverse: a sudden, militarily decisive, heavily punitive uprooting of all forms of local Protestantism, perfectly symbolised by the Habsburg ruler's physical tearing-up of the famous Bohemian charter of religious liberties, the Letter of Majesty. In Hungary the change began almost like Poland's, but ended almost like Bohemia's.

In Poland, important magnates began returning to their ancestral Catholicism in the 1560s, when the son of a Radziwill who had introduced the Reformation in Lithuania, the son of a Calvinist Grand Marshal of Little Poland, and the nephew of the Reformed leader John Laski all converted. This trend accelerated during the long reign of Sigismund III (1587–1632), where it can be seen most clearly in the shrinkage of the Protestant faction within Poland's principal governmental organ, the Senate. In 1586 Poland had thirty-eight Protestants among about eighty-five senators; in 1606, when an insurrection broke out (headed by a zealous Catholic but including Protestant sympathisers) there were only seventeen Protestant senators; and when Sigismund III died only six were left. This king adopted an informal but effective policy of refusing to name Protestants to important positions, while rewarding converts.

Table 8.1[11] *Political leaders of Great Poland, 1587–1632*

Type of official	Protestants	Catholics*	Unknown	Total
(locally elected)				
District official	20	20 (2)	9	49
Gentry official	10	15 (4)	5	30
(royally appointed)				
Lesser senators	16	35 (6)	5	56
City *starostas*	8	16 (2)	3	27
Great senators	7	26 (7)	2	35

* Catholic converts in parenthesis.

The activities of the Jesuits and the absence of a Polish Protestant university also contributed to Sigismund's long-run success in eroding Protestantism's magnate base. Even so, social relations between Protestants and Catholics remained cordial. Sigismund III had a younger sister who became a lifelong Lutheran, yet remained on good terms with him and received a full-dress state funeral; his most trusted adviser, Chancellor Zamoyski, was a Catholic who married four times, twice to Calvinists. One can discover Protestant and Catholic noblemen collaborating on anti-Jesuit propaganda, while Protestant printers published Catholic books. Even the paper used by the antitrinitarian press in Rakow came from a factory operated by Cistercian monks. From the court down to the world of printers, Sigismund III's Poland still boasted an easy going religious coexistence – and we should not forget that this ruler also ended the harassment of his Orthodox subjects, and carefully upheld the full legal privileges of Poland-Lithuania's numerous Jews.

The first Protestant group to experience serious and effective persecution were the antitrinitarians, who were harassed by Protestants and Catholics alike in the 1640s. Lutheran Danzig expelled its leading Polish Brethren in 1644, three years before the Polish Diet closed their schools and print-shops. In 1648, the mayor of Danzig and a Catholic Prussian bishop jointly proposed to exclude the antitrinitarians from the protection of the Warsaw Confederation. The move failed, but the next year the Diet excluded the Polish Brethren from participating in debates or serving in Parliament – at a moment, Polish historians remind us, when the Cromwellians were issuing the Draconian Ordinance of May 1648 which punished antitrinitarian propaganda with death. Ten years later, the Diet issued an ultimatum ordering all Brethren to convert or leave the kingdom within two years – the first important breach in Poland's tradition of religious freedom within the ruling class.[12]

Poland experienced two major catastrophes after 1648. The Cossack revolt of that year in the Ukraine meant not only the loss of the south-eastern part of the Polish state, but worse, a genuine war of religion in which Polish Catholics, Uniate Ruthenians, antitrinitarians and above all Jews were massacred. Seven years later the King of Sweden invaded Poland, nearly conquered it, and brought the 'deluge' to its peak. The successful recovery of most of the state made Catholicism into Poland's national religion (as it remains to this day, to an extent unique in east-central Europe), and made all forms of Protestantism suspect as disloyal, since the Lutheran invader had turned several churches over to native Protestants. Nevertheless, Protestants withered away in Poland rather than suffering any sudden extinction, apart from the antitrinitarians. Polish Protestants held synods and ran print-shops throughout the eighteenth century. Discrimination escalated when new Protestant churches were forbidden in 1716, and when Protestants were forcibly excluded from the Diet in 1718, but they never suffered anything like the persecutions of the French Huguenots. When Poland ceased to exist as a state in 1793, it still contained about seventy-five Protestant congregations, mostly in Lithuania.

Religious shift in the kingdom of Bohemia was sudden and total, except for Silesia. The battle of the White Mountain outside Prague in 1620 ended the rebellion of the Bohemians, and gave their Habsburg ruler an opportunity to eradicate Bohemian Protestantism. The follow-through was rapid and decisive. Protestant worship was prohibited, and the properties of all important participants in the rebellion were confiscated. The amount of land which changed hands in Bohemia in the late 1620s was without parallel in European history, at least since the Battle of Hastings in 1066: half of Bohemia's thousand noble estates, including 275 of the largest among them, were allotted new owners, so that over two-thirds of Bohemia's territory changed hands. At one stroke, Protestantism in the land of the Hussites had lost not just its churches but also its social base in the nobility. In 1627 the victorious Ferdinand ii expelled all non-Catholic nobles from Bohemia, whether or not they had participated in the rebellion: he extended this decree to Moravia in 1628. Although most now converted to Catholicism, about a quarter of the Czech nobility and leading burghers became exiles scattered throughout the Holy Roman Empire and beyond. They tried to return with Swedish armies during the later phases of the Thirty Years War, but were unsuccessful; a tightly-knit group of great magnate families, including several descendants of the 1620s profiteers, dominated Bohemia from the White Mountain until the nineteenth century.[13]

The situation in Hungary fell somewhere in between the Polish and Bohemian patterns of baroque Catholic reconquest. The differences were both chronological and geographical. The Catholic advance succeeded first and relatively peacefully in western and northern Hungary, where a few landed magnates were extremely powerful, and where Catholic proselytising had the full support of the Habsburgs. Even more than Bohemia or Poland, Hungary was the playground of a few, enormously wealthy, magnate families: as early as the 1550s, almost half the land in thirty-seven Hungarian countries belonged to only sixteen families. By 1600, all but a handful of Hungary's thirty or forty important clans were Protestant, while after 1650 only a handful remained so – particularly among the ten tightly intermarried aristocratic houses who controlled the local and national administration. There were few great estates in Transylvania, where Protestantism underwent a late, and relatively rapid, eclipse after the Diet acknowledged Habsburg sovereignty in 1690. Here, the repression of the Protestants soon provoked a serious rebellion in 1703–11, led by the heir to Hungary's second greatest estate, Ferenc II Rakoczi (one could travel for a hundred miles and never leave Rakoczi property). He was the grandson and great-grandson of the two most fanatical Calvinist princes of Transylvania, rulers who boasted of having read the Bible cover-to-cover thirty-seven times; but he was also the grandson of Zsofia Bathory, the last of a wealthy, famous and devoutly Catholic family who had converted Ferenc's father. His mother later remarried a Calvinist magnate, who led an abortive revolt against the Habsburgs in the 1680s. The 1703 revolt was led by Catholics like Rakoczi, but drew most of its support from Transylvania's Protestants, who made him their prince. After Rakoczi's defeat, Hungarian Protestants continued to survive in the eighteenth century, although they suffered under a 1691 law which placed their parishes under the supervision of Catholic bishops, and a 1731 law which made conversion from Catholicism a secular crime and forced Protestants to observe Catholic holy days. A Hungarian version of the English Test Acts, requiring officials to take oaths to the Virgin Mary and various saints, excluded practising Protestants from public posts. However, Hungary's population was still 15 per cent Calvinist at the time of Joseph II's 1786 census.[14]

Outside Bohemia and Moravia, some religious toleration remained in east-central Europe even at the height of the Counter-Reformation. Censorship was sporadic and incomplete. Freedom of expression was a cherished point of Hungarian liberties, and no Index of Prohibited Books was ever promulgated there. Poland acquired an Index in 1603, with two revisions before 1620; like its Roman or Spanish prototypes, it included superstitious and lascivious works as well as heretical titles. The best-known episode in Polish censorship came in 1627, when a nobleman drew a fine and six months' imprisonment for translating a work by a French Calvinist. The author neither paid his fine nor served his sentence, living undisturbed until the Polish Diet annulled his punishment in 1649. Although the antitrinitarians were prohibited from publishing in 1647 (as they had been in Transylvania since 1580), other Polish Protestants were at liberty to publish as long as the kingdom existed. In Bohemia, where all Protestant printers had been expelled in 1620, a copy of the Roman Index had appeared in Prague as early as 1596; but no specifically Bohemian Index was printed until 1729, and censorship remained haphazard.[15]

In Poland-Lithuania forebearance towards religious deviants occasionally gave way to prosecutions, and a few people were even killed for religious reasons: the greatest tensions involved Judaisers. A *bourgeoise* of Cracow was burned in 1539 for converting to Judaism; Christian servants were burned in 1556 and 1580 for delivering consecrated Hosts to their Jewish employers, who were also burned. (In Transylvania, where executions were even rarer, a Sabbatarian zealot was stoned to death by gypsies in 1639 for blasphemy.) Non-noble and foreign antitrinitarians also suffered: an Italian was drawn and quartered at Vilna in 1611 for preaching against the Eucharist; an antitrinitarian burgher was executed that year for trampling on a crucifix – but a Calvinist nobleman had gone unpunished for the same offence in 1580. The only nobleman to be executed for religious reasons before the 'Deluge' was an insane Catholic who had killed a priest and destroyed the Host during mass in 1588. Even afterwards, the only nobleman to suffer death was an atheist, beheaded at Warsaw in 1689. Polish historians insist that no Unitarians of noble birth ever suffered the full legal penalties even during the peak of the movement's repression. *De facto* Polish toleration went very far, especially for noblemen, who comprised a far larger share of the population here than in western Europe.[16]

But does this mean, as those historians claim, that Poland was a 'state without stakes' in the early modern era? One can find thousands of people burned at the stake for religious reasons in Poland, mostly after 1650: they were accused witches. Our best estimate suggests that Poland-Lithuania had about 10,000 witch trials in all, 70 per cent of them held after 1675, and nearly a third between 1701 and 1725. It seems as though Poland, reeling from the Cossack and Swedish invasions, sought its scapegoats for divine wrath not so much in the antitrinitarians as in those humble peasant women accused of becoming allies of Satan. The change of opinion was sudden. Polish Jesuits had opposed the use of torture on suspected witches at Lublin and Poznan in the 1630s (while approving the torture of a Calvinist troublemaker), but such scruples apparently vanished after the calamities twenty years later. Poland owns the dubious distinction of holding more witch trials than any other part of Christendom except the Holy Roman Empire, and its witch-hunts peaked much later than Germany's.[17]

The rest of east-central Europe was less brutal than Poland, but almost equally belated in staging its witch trials. Evidence from the kingdom of Bohemia suggests that persecution peaked here around the mid-seventeenth century, just after the Thirty Years War, and was most severe in the German parts of Silesia. The kingdom of Hungary, including Transylvania, had fewer than a thousand witch trials. Its witchcraft, like that of northern Protestantism, was centred on *maleficium* rather than on diabolical pacts, with few mass trials, only moderate amounts of torture, and numerous acquittals. The first known execution occurred at Calvinist-controlled Koloszvar/Klausenburg/Cluj in 1565, but Catholic areas staged the most Hungarian witch trials in the seventeenth and eighteenth centuries. In the Magyar zones, the statistical peak was not reached until the 1720s. Like Bohemia, where the worst outbreaks occurred along a 'militant perimeter' when teams of Jesuits proselytised to sullenly hostile villages in Silesia after 1650, in Hungary many witch trials took place in newly-recovered places, and there were close links in some of them between witchcraft and Protestantism, especially when defendants were charged with desecrating the Host.[18] By the end of the seventeenth century, the worst form of religious persecution in east-central Europe was this savage hunt for diabolists.

The great lesson which emerges from this overview of early modern east-central Europe is the reversability of toleration. In a region where noble privilege was strong, and central government was weak, a truly remarkable amount of peaceful coexistence flourished within all parts of the Christian community during the sixteenth century. Confessionalism generated much less friction here than in the Empire or in western Europe – at least until the 1600s. The hardening of religious intolerance came soonest and most violently in Bohemia, but the process was not confined to that kingdom nor to Catholics: in both Transylvania and Poland, Protestants led the fight against antitrinitarians. The persecution of witches, like the persecution of heretics, came late to this region. For Poland or Hungary, one could argue that the nadir of religious intolerance was not reached until c. 1725, with maximum legal disabilities against Protestants and maximum numbers of witch trials. By then, educated opinion in western Europe had reclassified witchcraft as a form of superstition, and was preparing an assault on intolerance by the 'enlightened'.

Notes

1 By far the best introduction is Alexander Giestyzor *et al., History of Poland*, 2nd edn (Warsaw, 1979), chs. 7–9. The author of that section, Janusz Tazbir, has also provided the best introduction to the religious history of early modern Poland, *A State Without Stakes: Polish Religious Toleration in the Sixteenth and Seventeenth Centuries* (New York, 1973).

2 The best introduction is now R. J. W. Evans, *The Making of the Hapsburg Monarchy, 1550–1700* (Oxford, 1979); see also Kenneth J. Dillon, *King and Estates in the Bohemian Lands 1526–1564* (Brussels, 1976), on Ferdinand's reign.

3 See E. Pamlényi (ed.), *History of Hungary* (London, 1975), chs. 1–4 (by L. Makkai); also the collaborative volume, *La Renaissance et la Réformation en Pologne et en Hongrie* (Budapest, 1963); and Stephen Bucsay, *Geschichte der Protestantismus in Ungarn*, vol. I (Vienna-Cologne, 1977). Quote from Dillon, 55.

4 Best general survey is Laszlo Makkai, *Histoire de la Transylvanie* (Paris, 1946); for the issue of toleration, Ludwig Binder, *Grundlagen und Formen der Toleranz in Siebenbürgen bis zur Mitte des 17. Jahrhunderts* (Cologne-Vienna, 1976).

5 Dillon, 68, 73–7, 144–5, 159, 167–73; Peter Brock, *The Political and Social Doctrines of the Unity of Czech Brethren in the Fifteenth and Early Sixteenth Centuries* (The Hague, 1957), 257–73.

6 Earl Morse Wilbur, *A History of Unitarianism*, 2 vols (Boston, 1945–52), II, 42–85, 106–15; see also Heinrich Fodor, 'Ferenc David, der Apostel der religiösen Duldung', *Archiv für Kulturgeschichte*, 36 (1954), 18–29; Binder, *Grundlagen*, 88–98, 152–5; and Massimo Firpo, *Antitrinitari nell'Europa orientale del '500* (Florence, 1977), 47–50, 75–94. The Sabbatarians became Nicodemites within the Reformed or the Catholic Church, emerging into daylight only in 1867 when Hungarian Jews received full civil rights and they formed themselves into a proselyte congregation of 136 people (Wilbur, II, 115).

7 Ambroise Jobert, *De Luther à Mohila* (Paris, 1974), 192–203; Tazbir, *State Without Stakes*, 80–1, 103–5, 108, 116, 192; Maria Bogucka, 'Towns in Poland and the Reformation', *Acta Poloniae Historica*, 40 (1979), 55–74.

8 Binder, *Grundlagen*, 99–123; Istvan Revesz, *La Réforme et les Roumains de Transylvanie* (Budapest, 1937).

9 Jobert, *Luther à Mohila*, 144, 148–52, 320–402, 405 (quote).

10 Evans, 109–10.

11 Taken from Edward Opalinski, 'Great Poland's Power Elite under Sigismund III, 1587–1632', *Acta Poloniae Historica*, 42 (1980), 62–3.

12 Wilbur, *Unitarianism*, I, 420–82; Tazbir, 121–7, 163, 177–80, 191, 201.

13 On the rebellion, see Hans Sturmberger, *Aufstand in Böhmen* (Munich-Vienna, 1959); one the repression, see K. Bösl (ed.), *Handbuch der Geschichte der Böhmischen Lander*, 4 vols (Stuttgart, 1967–74), II, 288–9, 292; and Josef Polishensky with Frederick Snider, *War and Society in Europe 1618–1648* (Cambridge, 1978), 202–16.

14 Etienne Szabo, 'Les grands domaines en Hongrie au début des temps modernes', *Revue d'histoire comparée*, n.s. 5 (1947), 172 n. 5; Evans, 240; Makkai, *Transylvanie*, 350–89; Bela Kiraly, 'The Hungarian Church', in W. J. Callahan and D. Higgs (eds), *Church and Society in Catholic Europe of the Eighteenth Century* (Cambridge, 1979), 107–108, 112–13.

15 Tazbir, 138–45, 171–3; Evans, 103–4, 346 n. 1.

16 Tazbir, 47, 76, 117–18, 199; Wilbur, *Unitarianism*, II, 116.

17 Bohdan Baranowski, *Procesy Czarnowie ew Polsce w XVII i XVIII wieku* (Lodz, 1952), summary in French; Tazbir, 192–3.

18 Evans, 400–15, esp. 406; Friedrich Muller, *Beitrage zur Geschichte des Hexenglaubens und des Hexenprocesses in Siebenbürgen* (Brunswick, 1854).

9 THE FACETS OF JUDAISM

Two of the most remarkable destinies in the history of Judaism belonged to men who were contemporaries, Baruch Spinoza (1632–77) and Sabbatai Zevi (1626–76). 'These two men', Martin Buber once noted, 'mark a late-exilic catastrophe of Judaism: Spinoza, a catastrophe in spirit and in his influence on Gentile nations; Sabbati Zevi, a catastrophe in life and in his influence on Judaism's inner structure'.[1] To an outsider, it seems more pertinent to observe that their parallel destinies represent extremes of thought and behaviour exceeding anything which existed in the far larger Christian community during the seventeenth century. No Christian philosopher surpassed or even equalled Spinoza's rational atheism for another century. No Christian chiliast ever had the immediate international impact of the most famous false Messiah. For all its vastness, the world of early modern Christendom offered less dramatic extremes of rationalism and superstition than the million or more Jews who lived among them.

A Sephardic Jew, born in the 'Dutch Jerusalem', Spinoza was seduced away from his Talmudic studies by the Cartesianism which flourished in the open society of Holland. Long before he began to study Latin in 1652, his Amsterdam Sephardic community had quarrelled over whether heretics and apostates suffered eternally; some freethinkers had argued that Christians, even Jesus of Nazareth himself, might eventually be saved. A notorious sceptic like Uriel da Costa (author of a Latin autobiography) was publically whipped for disbelief before committing suicide in 1647; a close friend and probable mentor of Spinoza, Juan de Prado, was put under rabbinic ban with Spinoza in 1656 for 'unspeakable blasphemies', but unlike him was eventually reconciled to Judaism. The most prominent Rabbi who refuted such heretics, Menasseh ben-Israel, was successfully negotiating the Jews' return to England at the moment of Spinoza's ban.[2]

After separating from Judaism, Spinoza lived among an obscure sect of radical Dutch Protestants, but never underwent baptism. He survived as a recluse on small pensions from a few Christian patrons, and supplemented his income by grinding lenses. During his lifetime he published only the *Principles of Descartes' Philosophy* in Latin and Dutch (1663) and the anonymous *Tractatus Theologico-Politicus* (1670). The latter was a combination of two polemics, loosely tied together by a general attack on 'superstitions'. One was announced in its sub-title: 'That Freedom of Thought and Speech ... may not, without Danger to Piety and Public Peace, be Withheld'. It amounted to an apologia for the bland religious toleration pursued by De Witt's republican administration. Spinoza's treatise became *Politicus* in the final five of its twenty chapters, which sharply attacked monarchical governments. Using the Old Testament, he claims (c. 18) that the Jews had only one brief civil war while they were a republic, but suffered almost continuous rebellions after becoming a monarchy. His final chapter is a ringing defence of freedom of speech in a free state, based on the history of Amsterdam's Counter-Remonstrants. It maintained that 'the real disturbers of the peace are those who, in a free state, seek to curtail the liberty of judgment which they are unable to tyrannise over'. Spinoza's defence of toleration was as extensive as Bayle's and broader than Locke's; it was also more doctrinaire than either, and therefore less influential.

Spinoza's other polemic was more remarkable than his defence of republican religious toleration. Most of his treatise was *Theologico*, directed against 'superstitions' and cast in the form of a commentary on the Old Testament; one of the earliest translations was entitled *Traité de la superstition des juifs, tant anciens que modernes*. He had relatively little to say about the New Testament. 'Although it was published in other languages, yet its characteristics are Hebrew' (ch. 7); the Apostles were teachers but not prophets, and they taught the true core of Biblical religion, 'obedience to God in singleness of heart, and the practice of justice and charity' (ch. 1); The New Testament contains contradictions, like the emphasis on salvation by faith in Romans and on salvation by works in James (ch. 11). But Spinoza's basic concern was the Old Testament (which, after all, forms about 75 per cent of the Christian Bible), undeniably composed in a language he knew well, and by a people he knew well.

Spinoza's interpretation of Scripture was more rational, sceptical and modern than that of his Christian contemporary, Richard Simon. Spinoza flatly denied the Old Testament miracles. 'A miracle . . . is a mere absurdity; what is meant in Scripture by a miracle is a work of nature which . . . is believed to surpass human comprehension' (ch. 6). He gave a lengthy demonstration proving why Moses could not have written the Pentateuch (chs 8–10); Job was 'a gentile, and a man of very stable character' (ch. 10); some minor prophets were also gentiles, and many of them prophesied to gentiles (ch. 3). The *Tractatus* contained a scandalous attack on Biblical prophets, who taught sound moral doctrine but were sometimes ignorant about scientific matters. Joshua ignored heliocentric theory; Solomon didn't know the ratio between the radius and the circumference of a circle; and Ezra couldn't even add correctly. Spinoza vehemently denied Jewish claims to be a chosen people distinguished by particular rituals and ceremonies. 'At the present time, there is absolutely nothing which the Jews can arrogate to themselves beyond other people.' But he continued 'that they have been preserved in great measure by gentile hatred, experience demonstrates.' Spinoza's criticisms sounded much like those of orthodox Christians, until he added that Jesus probably did not start such rituals as baptism or communion, which have nothing more to do with blessedness than does circumcision (ch. 5). In Moses' time, the Hebrews were primitive desert tribes, recently removed from slavery, who needed such ceremonies and laws to start them on the path towards true morality. But after the collapse of the Hebrew state, such props were no longer necessary or sufficient to ensure true religion. The Hebrew language, and the Hebrew nation, have lost their pristine grace and beauty (ch. 7).

Spinoza remained suspended between the Jewish community which had expelled him and the Christian community which he never joined. His posthumous works, collected and published by Christian admirers, included his notorious *Ethics*, which reinforced his reputation as an atheist, although they contained the word 'God' on every page (it is always *Deus sive Natura*, 'God alias Nature', and Spinoza really meant the latter). Spinoza also left behind an almost complete *Compendium of Hebrew Grammar*, which he tried to reduce to a set of 'geometrical' propositions like his other formal treatises, in order to demonstrate that Hebrew was a far more orderly and regular language than most scholars believed. Truly a solitary philosopher, a man without a family and without a Church, Spinoza was too radical for his own time, and even for the Enlightenment. He was refuted posthumously not only by 'progressive' Christians like Bayle, but also by 'progressive' Jews like Orobio de Castro. Christians began accepting him as a major philosopher in the nineteenth century; Jews finally lifted his excommunication in Palestine in 1932.[3]

Like Spinoza, Sabbatai Zevi was excommunicated by the Rabbis of a major Jewish community, but otherwise he inhabited an utterly different universe.[4] Born into a mercantile family of Smyrna on the Sabbath, hence his name, he was destined for the rabbinate. He had a decent education, but no literary skill; he wrote no treatises, not even an opinion on any point of Talmudic law. He composed only brief glosses on his copy of the kabbalistic *Zohar* which, according to the greatest student of Jewish mysticism, 'do not amount to much'. Charisma alone made him unusual. He was dignified, almost regal in appearance and bearing, yet natural in his dealings with all sorts of people – and occasionally seized by fits of manic ecstasy during which he did many bizarre things and broke many orthodox traditions. Some of his excesses were harmless, such as marrying himself to the Torah under a bridal canopy; others, such as arbitrarily changing the dates of major festivals, were more serious. For such scandals he was excommunicated by the rabbinate of Jerusalem in 1663. Yet he had followers in Palestine who accepted his innovations and believed his 'illuminations' were divinely inspired. One of them, Nathan of Gaza, became the major prophet of this group in May 1665 after persuading Sabbatai that he truly was the Messiah. Preceded by Nathan, Sabbatai made a triumphal return to Smyrna where he gained control of the Jewish community in December 1665. He reorganised the liturgical calendar, celebrating the Sabbath on Monday; he uttered the Ineffable Name of God in public repeatedly; he appointed at least twenty-one kings, headed by his two brothers. His reign in Smyrna was accompanied by a deluge of over 200 prophets of both sexes, led by some of his Palestinian followers, his wife, and even by the daughter of his most obdurate local enemy (who soon converted and became King Jeroboam).

The Messiah's arrival impressed and alarmed the outside world. Sabbatai departed for Istanbul just as the Sultan's government sent an order to Smyrna for his arrest. He was captured in the Dardanelles and imprisoned for seven months, while conflicting rumours and expectations flew around the Jewish world from Yemen to the Ukraine. The Messiah held many interviews and retained his royal bearing in prison. Rabbinic emissaries from Poland learned that there, but nowhere else, the persecutions of the Jews would be avenged. Sabbatai's adventure ended as farce rather than tragedy when the Sultan, in a personal interview, offered a choice between putting a turban on his head or chopping it off. Sabbatai converted. A note to his brother in Smyrna requested, 'Let me alone, for God had made me a Turk. Your brother, Mehemed *kapici bashi oturak*.'

However, Sabbatai Zevi's career, and even his influence, did not end with his apostasy. Nathan of Gaza continued to explain the mysterious mission of the Messiah, who had to be humbled in unforeseen ways; and a minority of his followers remained faithful. Sabbatai himself alternated between manic moods, during which he visited a dervish poet in Istanbul and proselytised for Islam in Spanish and Hebrew letters, styling himself 'the Master of Truth and Faith, the Turco and Mesurman', and depressive returns to his mystical Judaism. Amidst rumours that he had relapsed, the Sultan banished him to Greece in 1673. Sabbatai continued to live as a hybrid Jewish Muslim, signing himself 'the anointed of the God of Israel and Judah, Sabbatai Mehemed Şevi', although his final letter was signed 'the Messiah of the God of Israel and Judah'. Soon after his death, around 1685, the largest Jewish community in the world spawned an organised sect of Sabbatarians who professed Islam, but secretly worshipped as Jews. The Donmeh of Salonika survived until 1925, when they chose repatriation to Turkey, while much of their archives ended in Jerusalem: ultimately their bodies went to Islam but their papers went to Judaism.

Not all the significant Jewish destinies of the 1600s were excommunicated. In some respects, the career of the Marrano polemicist Fernando (Isaac) Cardoso (1604–83) was as important and interesting as either Spinoza or Zevi. In 1648, when Spinoza was still a rabbinical student and Sabbatai Zevi had not yet left Smyrna, Fernando Cardoso – sometime lecturer in philosophy at

Valladolid, physician in Madrid, poet, author of a treatise on Mount Vesuvius, a funeral oration for Lope de Vega, and medical works on the virtues of pure water and on intermittent fevers – secretly left Madrid and emerged in Venice, where he became a circumcised Jew, and renamed himself Isaac. By 1652 he had moved to Verona, where he served as physician to the Jewish community until his death. In his old age he published two major treatises: the first work of European philosophy by a practising Jew in over a century, the *Philosophia Libera* (Venice, 1673); and the most comprehensive and successful apologia for Judaism in many centuries, *Las excelencias de los Hebreos* (Amsterdam, 1679).[5]

Both periods of Cardoso's life were filled with the cultural ambivalence and paradoxes of Spain's 'New Christians'. In Madrid, Fernando contributed a sonnet to embellish a work by the author of a treatise on the menstruation of Jewish males (Cardoso also treated him for haemmorrhoids); he eulogised Lope de Vega, a conventional anti-semite who attended one of Cardoso's lectures just before death. But a careful analysis of his Madrid publications showed that Fernando never cited the New Testament except to show that the Jews who gave wine with myrrh to the crucified Jesus were not torturers, but merciful and compassionate. On the other hand, Isaac the Italian Jew remained saturated with Christian scholarship when composing his two final works. His 'free philosophy' exudes a quaint atomism; although he knew and cited Galileo's *Dialogues*, Cardoso remained anti-Copernican. In the *Excelencias*, many of his authorities are either Greco-Roman pagans, Fathers of the Christian Church, or modern Iberian chroniclers and historians. Jewish sources were always cited in Spanish, except for Biblical texts. 'There is no real evidence', says his biographer, 'that he had, at best, more than a rudimentary ability to read post-Biblical Jewish texts in the original language'. To add to the ambiguities of his biography, Fernando/Isaac had a younger brother, Miguel, who accompanied him to Italy in 1648 and was renamed Abraham. If the older brother with the younger name was sedentary, the younger brother personified the wandering Jew, moving to Livorno, then Egypt, and Tripoli, back to Livorno (where he was excommunicated in 1676); and finally to the Ottoman empire. Abraham became a fervent disciple of Sabbatai Zevi, trying until 1668 to persuade Isaac to believe in the apostate Messiah. Issac revenged himself by composing a cynical account of Sabbatai's adventures near the end of his *Philosophia Libera*; however, realising that Sabbatai offered too much ammunition to the Christians, he omitted him from his *Excelencias*.

Sabbatai Zevi was probably an Ashkenazi, but Spinoza and Cardoso were Sephardic Jews. Many important aspects of Judaism in early modern Europe revolve around the history of the Sephardim rather than the more numerous Ashkenazim, beginning with the trauma, drama and misery of the Iberian events of the 1490s. When Ferdinand and Isabella, flushed with their military triumph over the Moors, decreed the expulsion of all practising Jews in 1492, their kingdoms held about 400,000 previously converted Jews (*conversos*, or 'New Christians') and 200,000 practising Jews among their 6 million subjects. During the crisis, an additional 50,000 Jews, including several Rabbis, became Christians. Among those who emigrated, the majority (about 100,000) moved to Portugal, where they overwhelmed the small (20,000) native Jewish community and became an important element in a kingdom of well under 2 million. Although Spain had established her notorious Inquisition to deal with converted Jews in 1478, Portugal had no fully functioning Inquisition until 1547 – half a century after the traumatic, mammoth, forced baptism of all Portuguese Jews in 1497. Once it got under way, however, the Portuguese Inquisition was even more thorough in harassing descendants of these forcibly converted ex-Jews than its better-known Spanish counterpart. The history of Sephardic Jewry from 1500 to 1800 is a story of very gradual and extremely painful assimilation, coupled with thoroughgoing discrimination and persistent persecution, in the Iberian peninsula; and of a massive Diaspora throughout the Mediterranean basin, and ultimately to northern Europe among those who wished to remain Jews.[6]

Many Iberian Sephardim ended up in the relatively tolerant Ottoman empire, where they spread the use of Ladino (a Spanish dialect written in Hebrew characters) throughout the eastern Mediterranean. The great disbeliever in Sabbatai Zevi's Smyrna was a Portuguese Sephardi, and the only ridicule of him in the Jewish world came from two Sephardic brothers in Italy who composed sarcastic poems before his apostasy and a parody of the Passover satirising him afterwards. On the other hand, the

Sephardi Abraham Cardoso, then living in Tripoli, was one of his major prophets, and the Sabbatarian sect ultimately took root in a Ladino-speaking community, Salonika. The possibilities for Iberian Sephardim in the Ottoman world were demonstrated by the famous case of Dona Gracia Mendes and her nephew Joseph Nasi, who emigrated from Lisbon to Antwerp about 1536, then moved to Italy, where they emerged as practising Jews and patronised a famous edition of the Hebrew Bible, and finally settled in Istanbul after 1553 where she helped create one of the outstanding sixteenth-century banks and he became a major Ottoman political adviser, ending as Duke of Naxos and the Seven Islands, sponsoring Jewish resettlement in Palestine, and generally living a career straight out of the Arabian Nights.[7]

Although the Ottoman empire was truly hospitable, the most important aspect of the Sephardic Diaspora from 1490–1550 was the extensive acculturation of Jews in Renaissance Italy. Their assimilation took some remarkable forms. There were exotica like David Reubeni, who rode to an official audience with Pope Clement VIII in 1525 on a white horse, accompanied by an escort of ten Jews, and rode back with letters of introduction to numerous Christian kings. Armed with these, he visited Portugal in 1528, but was finally imprisoned by Emperor Charles V in 1541 and died in a Castilian *auto da fé*. On a different level, eighty Jews were awarded degrees in medicine and philosophy by the University of Padua between 1517 and 1619. On yet another level, the Jewesses of sixteenth-century Italy, unlike their menfolk, had non-Biblical names like Laura, Imperia, Diamante, Virtudosia and even a few goddesses like Diana or Pomona. But Sephardic Jewry probably wielded its most important influence in Renaissance Italy in the realm of ideas. One important strand ran from Ficino's doctrine of neoplatonic love through Jewish commentaries on the Song of Songs like that of Johann Alemanno in the 1490s, and culminated in the famous *Dialoghi d'Amore* by the Sephardic physician and philosopher of Naples, Judah Abrabanel alias Leone Ebreo, printed in 1535. Another strand, perhaps even more important to Renaissance thought, was the attempted Christianisation of the Kabbala by Pico della Mirandola and his numerous successors. Although Pico's thesis that 'no science can more firmly convince us of the divinity of Christ than magic and the kabbala' was censured at Rome in 1490, Christian kabbalism continued to flourish in the early sixteenth century. Pico's illustrious German disciple Johann Reuchlin, the first born Christian to compose a Hebrew grammar, dedicated his *De Arte Kabbalistica* to Pope Leo x in 1517, explaining obscure scriptural passages through kabbalistic exegesis: the remarkable French visionary Guillaume Postel translated the *Zohar* into Latin (published 1558 at Mantua). Major Protestant leaders were hostile to the movement, as was the Counter-Reformation Papacy; but faint traces of it survived until 1677, when a German Rosicrucian published a *Kabbala Denudata*.[8]

The reciprocal exchange between Jew and Christian in Renaissance Italy can also be seen in the history of printing. In 1477, a Jewish printer in Naples published the first critical edition of Dante's *Divine Comedy*. Italy was also an early centre of Hebrew publishing: of approximately 150 known Hebrew incunabula, over two-thirds were printed in Italy, mainly by the Soncino family. The largest Hebrew press in Renaissance Italy was run by a born Christian, Daniel Bomberg of Venice (1516–48), whose major competitor was another Venetian Christian. The climax to this development was the first major translation of the Bible into Spanish, printed in two almost identical editions in Ferrara. One version, dated 1553, was dedicated to the Duke of Ferrara, edited by Duarte Pinel, and published for Jeronimo de Vargas. The other version bore a Jewish date, was dedicated to Dona Gracia Mendes, edited by Abraham Usque and published for Yom-Tob Athias (who were Pinel and Vargas).[9]

However, a number of important signs showed that the Jewish–Christian rapprochement in Renaissance Italy came to a sudden end about then. A violently reactionary Grand Inquisitor, Cardinal Carafa, prohibited the printing of the Talmud in 1553, ending the hopes of Italy's Christian kabbalists and leading to bonfires of Hebrew books in several Italian cities. As Pope Paul IV, Carafa arranged the legal massacre of twenty-four baptised *Marranos* at Ancona, and penned the large Jewish colony of Rome into a ghetto in 1555; he created ghettos in the other Papal cities of Ancona and Bologna in 1556, starting a movement which gradually spread to other Italian cities between 1570 and 1640. In Counter-Reformation Italy, Jews were no longer able to avoid punishment for crimes by turning Christian; while proselytising literature reached unprecedented heights—not without some effect if we can trust the figure of 2430 Jewish conversions at Rome between 1634 and 1790. The Italian picture was not uniformly bleak, however. Venice continued her tolerance of *Marranos* (Isaac Cardoso dedicated his *Philosophia Libera* to the Venetian magistrates), while the Grand Dukes of Tuscany created a free port at Livorno in 1593, whose inhabitants were exempted from the Inquisition and whose Jews were never confined to a ghetto (by 1790, Livorno's Jewish population equalled that of Rome or Venice). But Counter-Reformation Italy gradually lost its unquestioned leadership over the *Marrano* Diaspora in Christian Europe.[10]

After 1600, that primacy passed to two new Sephardic colonies in Protestant northern Europe: Amsterdam and Hamburg. Like Livorno, they were 'free' settlements without ghettos and of course without an Inquisition. Jewish liberty was still far from absolute in the Protestant world. Before granting official toleration to its Jews in 1611, Hamburg requested advice from four Lutheran theological faculties, who approved of Jewish settlements 'provided they live quietly and unobtrusively' (one added that Jews should be forbidden to circumcise Christians or employ Christian servants): Hamburg's Jews could not worship publically until 1650. The Amsterdam colony were originally arrested under suspicion of practising Catholicism in secret, but were soon granted more privileges than at Hamburg. This settlement became the 'Dutch Jerusalem'. Symbolically, its first Rabbi was hired away from Venice, whose community they soon surpassed in intellectual vigour. By 1612 Sephardic Jews were publishing in Spanish, and several hundred *Marrano* titles poured off Amsterdam's presses in the seventeenth and eighteenth centuries. Amsterdam was the capital of Jewish rationalist heresy in the age of Da Costa and Spinoza; it was also the home of the first Jewish newspaper, the *Gazeta de Amsterdam* (1675–90), and of two Jewish literary societies, the *Academia de los Sitibundos* ('the Thirsty') (1676) and the more famous *Academia de los Floridos* (1685). Jews were highly visible participants in the rapid commercial prosperity of both Hamburg and Amsterdam. Over forty Portuguese Sephardim (virtually the colony's whole adult male population) bought shares in the Bank of Hamburg at its foundation in 1619; Amsterdam's 'Portuguese' were equally active in that city's Exchange Bank, where they comprised 106 of its 1202 depositors by 1620, rising to

265 of 2031 depositors by 1661. Amsterdam Sephardim were also active on the Stock Exchange. One of them published the classical description of speculation in stock shares, under the apt title of *Confusion de Confusiones*, in 1688. They even became slaveholders in distant Dutch Guyana, where they built a handsome synagogue in the *Joden Savanna* in 1685.[11]

Despite their economic modernity, Amsterdam's Sephardim were less completely assimilated socially and intellectually than their ancestors had been in Renaissance Italy. They published no liturgical works in Dutch until the late eighteenth century, and did not mingle much with their host community outside the world of commerce. Their intellectual achievements, unlike their commercial adaptation, fit oddly into the Christian mainstream of seventeenth-century Europe. When Menasseh ben Israel began his propaganda war to have Jews readmitted to Cromwellian England in 1650, he argued that England, whose name in medieval Jewish literature meant 'the end of the Earth', would have to receive Jews in order to fulfil the prophecy of Deuteronomy 28: 64 – that the dispersion of the Jews must be universal, 'from one end of the earth even unto the other' – and prepare the way for the Messiah. Even his far greater pupil, Spinoza, was a Cartesian rationalist who lacked Descartes' formal training in mathematics. 'Spinoza's confidence in crypto-mathematical reasoning in his ontology ... stems from the fact that unlike the great Christians Descartes, Leibniz or Newton, he had no genius of invention in this domain. His confidence in geometrical reasoning is of a mystical order.' No great Jewish mathematicians, no major Jewish natural scientists, therefore no truly central early modern thinkers emerged from the Dutch Jerusalem.[12]

In the Catholic Mediterranean world, for example in Venice, the Iberian Sephardim were often latecomers who created their communities alongside the already established German Ashkenazim; but in the Protestant north, at Amsterdam and later London, the Sephardim were the original Jewish settlers. Although both Sephardim and Ashkenazim used Hebrew as a liturgical language, they spoke different languages in everyday life, had different manners and customs, invariably maintained separate synagogues, and rarely intermarried. At Venice they even had separate ghettos. The Sephardim, who came from societies where most Jews had undergone Christian baptism (in Spain after 1391 or 1492, in Portugal after 1497), were already partially assimilated into the larger Christian community from which the Ashkenazim continued to be excluded. Thus in early modern European history the Sephardim were always the first 'modernisers', they learned Latin earlier, smoked tobacco sooner, adopted 'western' standards of decorum in their synagogues first. Moreover, Sephardim were usually richer than Ashkenazim, at least in Protestant Europe. In 1744, Amsterdam's 3000 Sephardim paid an average tax of 6 guilders; the Christian majority averaged 1.63 guilders; and the 10,000 Ashkenazim averaged only 0.32 guilders. One understands why the eighteenth-century Dutch Sephardi, Isaac de Pinto, objected that Voltaire's anti-semitic remarks might apply to Ashkenazim, but not to his people; even the dogmatically egalitarian French Revolution gave civil rights to its Sephardic Jews at Bordeaux and Bayonne a full year before granting them to the Ashkenazim of Alsace and Lorraine.[13]

It is equally important to recognise that throughout early modern Christendom 'Jewry' meant precisely this mixture of Sephardim and Ashkenazim. At Venice or Amsterdam, both communities were under the same legal system *vis-à-vis* Christians, with minor exceptions. Both communities were affected by the same currents of thought in the Jewish world. The excitement of Sabbatai Zevi's Messiahship illustrates how all Jews could be affected by the same events. At Hamburg, Glückl of Hameln described how the Ashkenazim ran to the Sephardic synagogue to hear the great news and see the younger Portuguese dressed up in green silk sashes, 'the colour of Sabbatai Zevi'. Hard-headed Sephardi and Ashkenazi merchants prepared to sail for the Holy Land, like Glückl's father-in-law who kept two enormous casks full of preserved food and clothing ready at Hamburg for three years. But Hamburg was also the home of an unemployed Rabbi, Jacob Sasportas, who later composed the most damning Jewish account of the false Messiah, the *Quissur Sisath Nobel Sevi* (first published at Amsterdam in 1737, but suppressed by that city's Sephardic congregation). His son carefully concealed the fact that even Sasportas – who preached a highly unpopular sermon in September 1666 attacking Sabbatai 'who wants to found a new religion, like Jesus' – had believed earlier that year in the authenticity of the Messiah. By March 1666 a solemn prayer for the new King of Israel was incorporated into regular Sephardic

Sabbath service. A former *Marrano* hastily printed a collection of
his Sabbatarian sermons in Hamburg in August 1666, under the
provocative title *Fin de los Dias*; the entire edition was confiscated
by Portugese elders 'until the hoped-for time which God may
bring nigh speedily'. Under the impact of Messianic tidings,
Hamburg's Ashkenazi congregation settled its quarrel with the
suburban Altona Sephardim over their joint burial ground, adding
to the public document signed before Christian magistrates a secret
clause to the effect that should redemption occur before Hamburg
paid its debt to Altona in full, the balance would be donated
towards the rebuilding of the Temple. Even a Hamburg
Ashkenazi rotting in prison in Oslo in 1666 received four letters in
Yiddish from his friends, telling him the great news. Few places are
so well documented as Hamburg, and no other episode of early
modern Jewish history cast such a blinding glare on both Sephardi
and Ashkenazi behaviour. Still, such evidence illustrates how both
major wings of Judaism shared much common ground, especially
in a strictly religious context.[14]

When we shift our attention to the Ashkenazi after 1500, we
enter a significantly different world. Its geography is dominated
not by a Diaspora but by a *drang nach Osten*. The dominant motif of
Ashkenazi history is the combination of expulsions from central
Germany in the sixteenth century, largely under the impetus of the
Lutheran Reformation, and the open-handed protection offered to
them by the rulers of Poland-Lithuania from Sigismund I
(1507–48) to Ladislas IV (1632–48). After 1500, the Ashkenazi
world shifted its centre of gravity from Germany to Poland, where
it remained until the time of the Nazis. The size of Jewish
settlement in Poland-Lithuania has been estimated by Salo Baron,
who calculated only about 30,000 Jews among its 5 million
inhabitants in 1500. By 1576, the Jewish population had increased
to 150,000 in an enlarged state with a total population of 7.5
million. By 1648 it had risen to 450,000 Jews in a still larger state
of 10 million: the ratio of Jews to total population in Poland-
Lithuania, 4.5 per cent, was by far the largest anywhere in
Christendom after 1497. After the Cossack massacres, the
Ashkenazi population fell to about 350,000 by 1660; but by the
time of Poland's first general census in 1764, the kingdom held
some 750,000 Jews among a population of 11.4 million (6.6 per
cent). In the mid-eighteenth century, nearly twice as many Jews

lives in Poland-Lithuania as in Austria-Hungary and the Holy Roman Empire combined; and roughly eight times as many Jews lived in Poland as in the Atlantic states of Holland, France, and England.[15]

Two other aspects of the Ashkenazi experience in Poland-Lithuania after 1500 also deserve emphasis. First, this vast settlement was not concentrated in urban ghettos in western Poland. Places such as Cracow or Poznan had important Jewish communities in the middle ages, which grew in size after 1500: Poznan's Jews lived in fourty-nine houses in 1530 and in 138 buildings by 1618. But Poland's new capital, Warsaw, long maintained its royal privilege *de non tolerandis judeis*, and in any event the majority of east European Jews had moved to the Grand Duchy of Lithuania. Even here, most were not in the few major towns, although the Lithuanian capital of Vilna held a synagogue by 1573 and in 1645 numbered 2600 Jews among 15,000 inhabitants. In Lithuania Jews settled along the 'moving frontier' in the south-east, especially after the permanent union of Lithuania with Poland in 1569. The far eastern Palatinates of Bratislav and Kiev held only two known Jewish communities in 1569, but had fifty (32,350 Jews) by 1648. In such White Russian centres as Smolensk, further north, Jewish settlement followed soon after Polish military occupation, and was later seriously threatened by Russian reconquest. The Ashkenazi in these regions were surrounded not by Polish Catholics, but by Orthodox Ruthenians and Ukrainians. Just beyond lay the lands of the Cossacks, who rose against their Polish suzerains in 1648, starting a bloody war which ultimately cost Poland-Lithuania its Ukrainian provinces, and Polish Jewry about a third of its people.[16]

The other major aspect of eastern European Ashkenazim after 1500 is that they remained more totally alien in Poland-Lithuania than their Sephardic counterparts in western Europe, or even their fellow Ashkenazim in Germany. Whether they lived among Catholics or Orthodox peasants, these Jews had minimal cultural interaction with their neighbours. Their Yiddish language remained remarkably unaffected by either Polish or Ukrainian loan words, except for a few technical terms from court procedures or other official transactions; because they were also unaffected by Luther's linguistic reforms, their mixture of old Germanic vocabulary and Hebrew religious-philosophical terms diverged

increasingly from the spoken German of the Empire. Another sign
of isolation is that Polish Jews seemed remarkably ill-informed
about the rich and complicated history of the Protestant Reformation in sixteenth-century Poland, in contrast to the rabbis of
Frankfurt or Prague. One must also realise that in Poland-
Lithuania there was remarkably little pressure on Jews to become
Christian, so that converts either to or from Judaism were
extremely rare. In formal disputation with Christians, a Jewish
spokesman claimed that 'no Jew changes his religion out of
conviction. Jews convert to Christianity in pursuit of pleasure,
from infatuation with a beautiful woman, or in order to be released
from debts'. Significantly, he did not recognise the possibility of
conversion through fear or coercion.[17]

Yet there were definite limits to the toleration which the
Ashkenazim of Poland enjoyed from their Catholic authorities and
neighbours. Jewish history in Poland-Lithuania was filled with
references to the 'blood libel', the accusation that Jews slaughtered
Christian children for ritual purposes. Such charges were
becoming rare in western Europe after 1500, and nearly all
Protestant leaders agreed with the Renaissance Papacy that the
blood libel was a ridiculous myth. In Poland, several royal decrees
granted full legal protection to Jews accused of ritually murdering
Christians; if the accuser could not produce three Christian and
three Jewish witnesses to the crime, he would suffer death himself.
However, in 1598 a Polish Jesuit compiled a list of no fewer than
thirty-four ritual murders and fourteen desecrations of the Host
committed by Polish Jews, nearly all of them recent. Nevertheless,
there were few outbreaks against Polish Jews before 1648. A riot
at Cracow in 1637 where seven Jews were killed (and thirty-three
converted in order to save their lives) was long commemorated by
a special day of mourning because of its unusual severity. The Jews
of Poland-Lithuania lived cautiously, trying to avoid all
provocations of their Christian neighbours. Whereas Isaac
Cardoso printed his *Excelencias de los Hebreos* in the West in 1679,
the greatest apologia for Judaism produced in Poland, completed
in 1595, first appeared in print in a 1681 refutation of Cardoso by a
Bavarian Catholic. In the sprawling state of Poland-Lithuania,
Jews were consistently protected by the monarchs, but royal
power was itself weak by western European standards; therefore
the Jews reinforced their traditional aloofness in order to reduce

their vulnerability. It is one of the minor paradoxes of Jewish history in early modern Europe that the state with the most Jews in it had perhaps the least amount of meaningful interaction between Jews and Christians.[18]

Considering the large numerical preponderance of Ashkenazim over Sephardim, it is not surprising that both major developments in eighteenth-century Judaism occurred among the former – one in Poland, the other in Germany. The Polish development was a strictly religious phenomenon, the creation and rapid growth of modern Hassidism. Polish Jewry, which had suffered so heavily from the Cossack massacres of 1648–55, was understandably deeply affected by the false Messiah of 1666, especially in the south-eastern provinces which had been devastated in 1648. Eventually this region spawned its own false Messiah, the sinister Jacob Frank, who used his chiliastic power to persuade about 2000 Jews to follow him voluntarily into Christian baptism around 1760. Another very different type of Jewish mysticism arose in nearby Galicia about 1750, where a small group of anti-Messianistic kabbalists withdrew to the *Klaus* of Brody to study and pray as 'Jewish Jansenists'. Much more important than either was the 'Jewish Methodism' of the 'Ashkenazi Wesley', the Baal-Shem Tov (1700–60) and his disciples or *zaddiks*. Its rapid success was explained by Gershon Scholem:

The first fifty years of Hassidism [1760–1810], its truly heroic period, are characterised by this spirit of enthusiasm which expressed and at the same time justified itself by stressing the immanence of God in all that exists. But this enthusiasm was . . . not based on chiliastic expectations. Here is the explanation of the fact that when it came into conflict . . . with the sober and somewhat pedestrian spirit of rabbinical orthodoxy, typified by the Lithuanian brand, it more than held its own.

Because the early Hassidim were founded by a layman with no rabbinical training, and led by disciples who shunned the scholarly study of the Torah, they could hardly fail to collide with the regular rabbinical leadership headed by the Gaon Elijah of Vilna. Open conflict broke out in 1772, when the Gaon excommunicated and banished Vilna's Hassidic chiefs for inserting Yiddish words into their prayers, or turning somersaults in public. The Gaon had identified some of the movement's strengths – its penchant for pithy Yiddish epigrams and aphorisms, and its anti-intellectual enthusiasm. Thus began a fight which ended in 1804 when the Imperial Russian government (not otherwise noteworthy in the history of Jewish toleration) deprived the rabbinate of the right to banish religious dissenters. The Hassidim, for their part, soon began of ossify into a sect of hereditary charismatic *zaddikis*. Their worst defect was a total lack of fresh religious ideas or theories of mystical knowledge even among its first generation of mystic saints. Such an acute and fundamentally sympathetic critic as Scholem noted that in all other forms of Jewish mysticism 'it was always possible to lay down a blueprint . . . of the spiritual architecture of the subject-matter; but in the case of Hassidism we cannot do so'. But the remarkable achievement of that first generation of mystics and epigrammatists suffices to place Hassidism among the principal achievements of eighteenth-century Judaism. It has, after all, inspired a Nobel laureate.[19]

Considering the extent of Sephardic assimilation in Holland and England, it is noteworthy that the most important movements for the acceptance of Jews into gentile society during the Enlightenment took place not in the Atlantic states, but in Germany. Except for prolonged, but only marginally successful, efforts by English Sephardim to join Masonic lodges, there was no significant Jewish acculturation in the capitals of the Enlightenment before the age of the French Revolution. The British Freemasons ended by developing the Scottish Rite, which excluded practising Jews; the British Parliament quickly repealed the 'Jew Bill' of 1753, which would have allowed a few of the richest immigrant Sephardi to become naturalised through private Acts of Parliament. In France, a handful of 'liberated' young Jews in Paris kept gentile mistresses, and one young Sephardi fought a duel with a French police inspector; but the crown prince of French *philosophes*, Voltaire ridiculed Judaism as an even grosser form of superstition than Christianity, and most of his peers agreed.[20]

The major breakthrough in Jewish-Gentile relations in eighteenth-century Europe occurred in the Berlin of Moses Mendelssohn (1729–86). For thirty years this remarkable man managed to participate fully in the intellectual life of the Prussian capital while remaining a practising Jew, skilfully avoiding both a rupture with the Rabbis and efforts to convert him into either a Christian or a Deist. His life gave new meaning to the old Jewish slogan that 'from Moses to Moses [Maimonides] there was no one like Moses'.

He maintained a lifelong friendship with Lessing, who apparently used him as a model for *Nathan der Weise*. Mendelssohn achieved literary notoriety by winning the 1763 essay competition of the Berlin Royal Academy, edging out a young unknown named Kant, and reinforced his fame with his dialogue *Phädon* (1767) which defended the immortality of the soul. The major work of his later years was a German translation of the Torah, which finally appeared in 1782. He followed it with a treatise called *Jerusalem ; or On Religious Power and Judaism*, in 1783. Mendelssohn remained in the mainstream of the German *Aufklärung*, faithful to the philosophy of Leibniz and Wolff, distrusting the French *philosophes* as superficial, and proclaiming himself too old to understand Kant by the 1780s. He was more successful in bringing Haskalic or 'enlightened' Judaism to the attention of German gentiles than in bringing the wisdom of the gentiles to the Jews.[21]

Mendelssohn was neither the only, nor even the first, 'enlightened' Ashkenazi; like Spinoza, he had his less famous predecessors and contemporaries. Two German Rabbis, thirty years older than he, had a thorough knowledge of contemporary gentile achievements in natural science and in philosophical rationalism. Mendelssohn began wearing a wig in 1759, twenty years after another Berlin Jew had created a major scandal by appearing in synagogue with a wig and without a beard (Mendelssohn preferred a small, neatly-trimmed beard). Mendelssohn tried to launch a liberal periodical in Hebrew in 1758, but quit at once; a successful Hebrew journal was founded in 1783, which moved to Berlin the year Mendelssohn died, and published until 1811. One of Mendelssohn's contemporaries, an Amsterdam Rabbi, complained in 1772 that both Ashkenazim and Sephardim used razors, attended the theatre and the opera, sent their children to universities, and generally lived dissolute lives. But not only Ashkenazi men adopted eighteenth-century high fashion. Almost as important as Mendelssohn, and far more colourful, were the Jewish salon hostesses at the heart of Berlin society in the 1790s. By a reversal of the usual social logic which makes women the primary guardians of tradition, the Jewesses of Berlin mixed more easily than their brothers in gentile society, partly because they had no Hebrew education in Torah to unlearn. The most famous of Mendelssohn's children, married at eighteen to a proper Jewish youth, had a glittering social career. She eventually deserted her husband for a Bohemian intellectual, and turned Catholic in Paris in order to marry her lover. Three of her five siblings converted to Lutheranism; her best friend, the *salonière* Henriette Herz, also ended as a Catholic convert. Such were the social rewards and religious perils of Jewish emancipation.[22]

The world of European Jewry still contained remarkable extremes at the end of the eighteenth century. It is a very long way indeed from the somersaulting enthusiasm of the early *zaddiks* to the elegantly fashionable Berlin or Vienna salons where Christian noblemen and intellectuals mingled under the watchful eyes of Jewish hostesses. It seems a long way from either of these images to the final outpost of the Sephardic Diaspora, the sober and symmetrical synagogue of 1763 which still stands in Newport, Rhode Island, built with the help of Portuguese *Marranos* who had fled Lisbon after the famous earthquake of 1755. But remarkable as these differences are, they seem less glaring than the distance between Spinoza and Sabbatai Zevi a century before. Mendelssohn was less daring, and therefore more successful, than Spinoza had been. The Baal-Shem Tov and his disciples were less pretentious, and therefore more successful, than the Sabbatarian heretics.

In several important ways the eighteenth century was no improvement on the sixteenth in terms of Christian-Jewish relations. The eighteenth century had its court Jews, a lengthy process whose social culmination came when Solomon Rothschild became a Baron of the Austrian Empire in 1823; but he glitters no brighter than the Lisbon-born banker who had become Duke of Naxos and the Seven Island 250 years earler. The eighteenth century had Mendelssohn and Lessing's *Nathan der Weise*; but the sixteenth had Judah Abrabanel's doctrine of neoplatonic love, and the prolonged effort to Christianise the kabbala. In both centuries Jews were granted degrees, primarily in medicine, by Christian universities. Even two people as utterly different as the enlightened despot Joseph II, 'Reason Enthroned', and the most reactionary Counter-Reformation Pope, Paul IV, shared an identical policy towards the Talmud. Joseph II forbade its study in a decree of 1785 (four years after his Edict of Toleration) 'in order that the Jews, who believe in stupid exorcisms of the Devil and in all manner of similar follies, may at least not continue to persist in such nonsense and thereby risk either postponing or entirely losing education and enlightenment'; the then Grand Inquisitor had merely ordered all

Talmudic books destroyed. The 'emancipation' of European Jewry made few important advances – particularly in terms of Christian sensitivity to Jewish culture – until long after the French Revolution had begun the process of Jewish enfranchisement and official de-Christianisation.[23]

Notes

1   Martun Buber,'Spinoza, Sabbati Zevi and the Baal-Shem', in his *Origins and Meaning of Hassidism* (New York, 1960), 90 (first published 1927 as foreword to Buber's *Die chassidischen Bücher*).

2   On Spinoza's environment, see I.S. Revah, *Spinoza et le docteur Juan de Prado* (Paris-Hague, 1959); and Revah's 'La réligion d'Uriel de Costa, marrane de Porto', *Revue de l'histoire des réligions*, 161 (1962), 45–76; and Cecil Roth, *Menasseh ben Israel* (Philadelphia, 1934).

3   See Leo Strauss, *Spinoza's Critique of Religion* (New York, 1965); the best critical edition of the *Tractatus* is by Carl Gebhardt (Heidelberg, 1926). The French title is in Kingma-Offenburg-Van Eeghen, 'Bibliography of Spinoza's Works up to 1800', *Studia Rosenthalia*, 11 (1977), 18–19 (15).

4   Gershon Scholem, *Sabbatai Sevi, the Mystical Messiah 1626–1676* (Princeton, 1973), esp. 154, 128, 423, 686, 681 n. 263, 840–1, 915–17. ⌐he Turkish phrase means 'honorary keeper of the palace gates', a sinecure which the Sultan awarded to the new convert.

5   Yosef H. Yerushalmi, *From Spanish Court to Italian Ghetto. Isaac Cardoso: A Study in Seventeenth-Century Marranism and Jewish Apologetics* (New York, 1971), esp. 184–6, 136, 154, 159–60, 365, 343–9.

6   The basic survey is Cecil Roth, *A History of the Marranos*, 4th edn (New York, 1974); also I.S. Revah, 'Les marranes', *Revue d'études juives* 108 (1959), 29–77.

7   Scholem, *Sabbatai Sevi*, 395–8, 516–18, 696–7; see the twin biographies by Cecil Roth: *The House of Nasi: Dona Gracia* (Philadelphia, 1947), and *The Duke of Naxos* (Philadelphia, 1948).

8   See both Cecil Roth, *The Jews in the Renaissance* (Philadelphia-New York, 1959), and Moses I. Shulvass, *The Jews in the World of the Renaissance* (Leiden, 1973); also François Secret, *Les Kabbalistes chrétiens de la Renaissance* (Paris, 1964); on Reubeni, see Roth, *Marranos*, 68, 148–9.

9   Roth, *Renaissance*, 162–88; Roth, *Marranos*, 324–5.

10   The best survey of post-Tridentine Italy is Salo W. Baron, *A Social and Religious History of the Jews*, 2nd edn, 16 vols (New York,

1952–76), xiv, 71–146; see also Kenneth Stow, *Catholic Thought and Papal Jewish Policy, 1555–1593* (New York, 1977).

11 See Roth, *Marranos*, 229–51, 343–59; Baron, xiv, 271–85 (Hamburg); xv, 3–74 (Amsterdam).

12 Roth, *Marranos*, 262; quote from Pierre Chaunu, *La Civilisation de l'Europe classique* (Paris, 1966), 523.

13 Baron, xv, 53; Arthur Hertzberg, *The French Enlightenment and the Jews* (New York, 1968), 180–3, 338–68.

14 Scholem, *Sabbatai Sevi*, 566–91, 934, 991; Glückel of Hameln, *Memoirs*, ed. M. Lowenthal (New York, 1932), iii, c. 2 (45–7).

15 On the Jews of Poland-Lithuania before 1648, see Baron, *Social and Religious History*, xvi (New York, 1976).

16 Baron, xvi, 182, 192, 208; Israel Cohen, *Vilna* (Philadelphia, 1943), 4–5, 99.

17 Baron, xvi, 7–8, 64–5, 72–4, 305; Cohen, *Vilna*, 73–4, mentions the conversion of a Lithuanian nobleman – but he converted in western Europe, and was burned at the stake when he returned to Poland in 1749.

18 Baron, xvi, 89–105, 147, 189. The basic Jewish narrative of the Cossack rising, Nathan Hannover's account, was printed in Hebrew at Venice in 1653.

19 See especially Gershon Scholem, *Major Trends in Jewish Mysticism*, 3rd edn (New York. 1954), 325–50 (quotes 336, 338); see also Cohen, *Vilna*, 227–52; G. Scholem, 'Le Mouvement Sabbatiste en Pologne', *Revue de l'histoire des religions*, 163 (1953), 30–90, 209–32.

20 See Jacob Katz, *Jews and Freemasons in Europe, 1723–1939* (Cambridge, Mass., 1970); Thomas W. Perry, *Public Opinion, Propaganda and Politics in Eighteenth-Century England: a Study of the Jew Bill of 1753* (Cambridge, Mass., 1962); Hertzberg, *French Enlightenment and the Jews*, 161, 268–313.

21 See Alexander Altmann, *Moses Mendelssohn* (Birmingham, Ala., 1973). A good brief sketch is in Jacob Katz, *Out of the Ghetto* (Cambridge, Mass., 1973), 47–64; see also Henri Brunschwig, *Société et romantisme en Prusse au XVIIIe siècle* (abridged edn, Paris, 1973), 107–61.

22 Altmann, *Mendelssohn*, 83–4, 96–9, 725–6; Katz, *Out of the Ghetto*, 34, 36, 56, 84, 86, 120, 125–6, 146–7, 236 n. 11; see also Michael Meyer, *The Origins of the Modern Jew* (Detroit, 1967), 102–14.

23 Baron, xiv, 29–32; Max Grunwald, *Vienna* (Philadelphia, 1936), 148–9.

EPILOGUE

'God preserve us', said Pierre Bayle in 1691, 'from the Protestant Inquisition! Another five or six years or so and it will have become so terrible that people will be longing to have the Roman one back again.' This irritated outburst from a man who had lost his teaching post in France less than ten years earlier, and would lose his post in Rotterdam two years later through the demands of rival orthodoxies, reminds us of the continuing strength of religious intolerance in 1700. There are several clues that the major Protestant confessions were every bit as intolerant of each other in 1700 as they had been in 1600, if not more so. It seems probable, for instance, that in England more ministers were deposed by either the Puritan rebellion of the 1640s or the Anglican restoration of the 1660s than had been removed when Mary Tudor restored Catholicism in the 1550s; even the Glorious Revolution of 1688 eventually forced many more English curates from their pulpits than had the Elizabethan restoration of the 1560s. In Scotland this discrepancy was greater still, with the Presbyterian restoration of the 1690s being by far the worst disaster for her incumbent parish clergy. Moreover, the dispossessed ministers of the seventeenth century received no pensions from the revenues of their former parishes, unlike the English monks or Scottish priests of the Reformation era. Henry Kamen assessed the English Toleration Act of 1689 as 'reactionary in tone and content', pointing out that it included no theory of toleration, repealed no existing statutes against religious liberty and even destroyed much religious liberty in British North America.[1]

If Protestant ecumenism was still a chimera in 1700, so was the ideal of peaceful coexistence between Protestants and Catholics. The well-known irenic negotiations between Leibniz and Bossuet seem even more futile than those between Melanchthon and

Contarini a century and a half earlier at Regensburg. The English government's Toleration Act of 1689 may have been misnamed, but not its Irish Penal Laws of the 1690s. The worst persecutions of German Calvinism occurred not during the horrors of the Thirty Years War, but in the 1690s, with a Catholic Elector and French troops in the Palatinate. Louis xiv's revocation of the Edict of Nantes in 1685 was not anachronistic, but – like so much else this monarch did – serves as an appropriate symbol for his age.

In the largest area of eastern Europe, the kingdom of Poland, historians agree that a 'golden age' of religious toleration in the sixteenth century was followed by a 'silver age' in the early seventeenth century, and then drowned in Poland's 'Deluge' after 1648. It is instructive to compare the Polish nobleman beheaded in 1689 for atheistic beliefs with the Polish nobleman who publically trampled on a crucifix a century before and got off scot-free. It is also instructive to recall that the worst religious massacres in eastern Europe, the Cossack rising which exterminated Jews on an unprecedented scale (as well as many Latin Christians and even Uniates unlucky enough to fall into their hands), occurred in the same decade as the worst massacres in western Europe, the uprising of Irish Catholics against Ulster Scots colonists. Eastern and western Europe were not always on different historical timetables in the matter of religious toleration, or the lack thereof, in early modern Europe.

The most significant victims of religious intolerance at all times in early modern Europe were the Jews. For them, the Cossack massacres were by far the worst persecution they had suffered anywhere in Christendom for several centuries, certainly the first major pogrom since the Lisbon massacres of 1506. The history of Christian persecution of Jews in early modern Europe is dominated not by collective massacres, but rather by the slow yet steady harassment of the Iberian Sephardic remnant by the Spanish and Portuguese Inquisitions. Brutal at first in Spain, where several thousand converted Jews were killed within fifty years of the Inquisition's founding in 1478, the burnings slackened off considerably thereafter: about 500 Jews executed across a century and a half. However, these killings continued for an extremely long time; Judaisers were still being put to death by the Inquisition in Bourbon Spain in the 1720s and with somewhat more frequency by the Portuguese Inquisition in the eighteenth century. Printed pamphlets from Lisbon list thirty-one Judaisers killed at eighteen *autos de fé* between 1684 and 1720, and another 126 executed at twenty-two *autos* between 1723 and 1754. (Jews continued to comprise 85 per cent of Lisbon's cases in both periods.) At least from the point of the Sephardic Jews, the eighteenth century brought precious little 'enlightenment' to Christians.[2]

In most parts of Christendom, apart from the Mediterranean Inquisitorial lands and Holland, more witches were killed during the early seventeenth century than before. In several places the zenith of witch-hunting occurred only during the second half of the seventeenth century. The parallel between Austria's *Zauberjäckl* witch trials (1675–81) and Sweden's greatest witch panic (1668–76) is striking. In the Duchy of Württemberg, the closest approximation to a witch panic occurred in 1683–4; while in British North America it happened slightly later, in 1692. The chronology of Polish and Hungarian witch trials suggests a statistical peak sometime around 1720. Even the Inquisitorial courts, which had abandoned the notion of executing witches a century before, were still busily trying people for many other forms of magical superstitions into the eighteenth century; in cynical and carnivalesque Venice, the largest annual total of people tried for illicit magic was reached in 1709, with nearly 200 indictments.

Intolerance and superstition thus spilled over into the eighteenth century. The Swiss were still fighting a religious civil war in 1713 (and killed a witch as late as 1782). Dutch Catholics were going through the painful motion of a Jansenist schism which was finally consummated in 1727, about the time that Scottish Presbyterianism was beginning its multiple schisms. The Archbishop of Salzburg expelled thousands of his Lutheran subjects in the 1730s; the Lisbon Inquisition stepped up its continuous crusade against 'New' Christians who were by then sixth- or seventh-generation Jewish converts. By 1730, the implementation of Tridentine reforms was almost complete within Catholicism, and the elimination of superstitions almost complete within Reformed Europe, but genuine religious toleration seemed as remote as ever, confessionalism as strong as ever.

It is against such a background that one must assess the

generation of Bayle, Bekker and Thiers, and also the men of the
high Enlightenment in the mid-eighteenth century. The central
fact about the former is that they lived in a time of extensive
religious persecution, both of rival sects and of witches. The
daring of Bayle and his contemporaries in questioning the
significance of comets or the powers of the Devil seems much
greater, considering their circumstances. At the same time, the
desire of Bayle of Bekker to remain orthodox Calvinists, or of
Thiers – tireless classifier of Catholic superstitions – to avoid
serious difficulties with his Church, testifies to the continuing
vitality of confessionalism within Christendom. The early
assaulters of superstition were not secessionists.

On the other hand, Voltaire and his Deistic counterparts
inhabited an era when overt religious persecution had slackened
among Christian churches, when confessionalism had lost much of
its vigour, and when the Devil himself seemed to have lost the
capacity to inspire terror. They could envisage a post-confessional,
perhaps a post-Christian Europe. They could cry, *Ecrasez l'infâme*!
and watch their campaigns actually work: Calas rehabilitated;
torture outlawed by all progressive governments; witch trials
almost extinct in western Europe and dying down even in the east;
the abolition, not of *l'infâme*, but of its strong right arm, the Society
of Jesus, in 1772; the epitome of enlightened despotism, Joseph II,
inheriting the Habsburg throne and launching literally thousands
of directives to reform religious life over much of eastern Europe.
The men of the high Enlightenment could and did firmly oppose
all kinds of intolerance and superstition – all except its most
socially acceptable form, anti-semitism. An 'enlightened' Ashkenazi from Metz complained in 1787 that

> people are writing and arguing much in France about tolerance, but what
> people are thinking about are only the various Christian sects. We are
> ignored, for the *philosophes* look on us as much too unimportant . . . . I do
> not know if in this philosophic century the prejudices against us are still
> believed, but I do know that we still feel their unrelenting effects.[3]

Only the French Revolution began implementing Bayle's great
insight that a full-fledged system of religious toleration for
Europeans involved not only peaceful coexistence among Protestants or between Protestant and Catholic, but also between
Christians and Jews.

Notes

1 Henry Kamen, *The Rise of Toleration* (London, 1967), 201, 211–12.
2 About ninety of these printed pamphlets, covering the three Portuguese tribunals between 1685 and 1760, are in the library of Hebrew Union College, Cincinnati, Ohio.
3 Arthur Hertzberg, *The French Enlightenment and the Jews* (New York, 1968), 330–1.

INDEX

175